THE DU GUIDE TO STARTING A BUSINESS

2024

Step-by-Step Blueprint to Build a Business not a Job| The Creative Business Handbook

FRANK REYNOLDS

TABLE OF CONTENTS

INTRODUCTION

A. The Importance of Entrepreneurship:
Unlocking Your Potential

In this introductory segment, we'll look into the relevance of entrepreneurship and its role in today's changing business world. As an expert in the business world, I intend to equip you, a beginner entrepreneur, with a complete grasp of the transforming force of entrepreneurship.

Entrepreneurship is the driving force behind innovation, economic development, and job creation. It helps people to bring their ideas into reality, disrupt industries, and have a beneficial effect on society. By adopting an entrepreneurial attitude, you can take charge of your future, question the status quo, and create possibilities for yourself and others.

Throughout this book, I will offer my skills and ideas garnered through years of experience in the business arena. My objective is to educate you with the information and skills required to traverse the exciting but complicated process of establishing your own company. Whether you're a student dreaming of founding a business, an ambitious entrepreneur seeking financial independence, or a person ready to follow your passion, this book will act as your compass.

By the end of this book, you will gain a solid foundation in the principles of entrepreneurship, learn how to generate and evaluate business ideas, create a comprehensive business plan, navigate legal and regulatory considerations, establish a strong brand and marketing strategy, master sales and customer acquisition techniques, efficiently manage operations and finances, overcome challenges and risks, and even plan for long-term success and growth.

Now, let's go on this adventure together, as we study the enormous world of entrepreneurship and enable you to develop your aspirations into a flourishing company enterprise. Get ready to unlock your potential, embrace innovation, and start on the road to entrepreneurial success.

B. Who is this Book for?
A Guide for Aspiring Entrepreneurs of All Backgrounds

This book is aimed to cater to the demands of prospective entrepreneurs from all backgrounds and experience levels. Whether you have a bright company concept blooming in your head or just the desire to explore the world of entrepreneurship, this book is for you.

1. Novice Entrepreneurs: If you're new to the entrepreneurial world and want direction on how to establish your firm, this book will give you a detailed path. It will break down difficult subjects into clearly comprehensible words, providing you with the essential knowledge to jumpstart your entrepreneurial path.

2. Students and Graduates: If you're a student or recent graduate pondering entrepreneurship as a career option, this book will provide you with the key information and skills necessary to transform your ideas into a successful company. You'll get insights into market research, financial management, marketing techniques, and more, establishing you on the correct course to entrepreneurial success.

3. Professionals Seeking position move: If you're an experienced professional wanting to move from your present position into

entrepreneurship, this book will give you essential insights and tactics to create a smooth changeover. It will help you learn the subtleties of beginning a company, managing money, and successfully promoting your goods or services.

4. Small company Owners: If you've already created a small company and want to take it to the next level, this book will give essential ideas on scaling, growth strategies, and operational efficiency. You'll discover how to overcome typical difficulties, adjust to shifting market dynamics, and improve your firm for long-term success.

5. Individuals with a Passion or Idea: If you have a passion or unique idea that you want to convert into a successful company, this book will assist you through the process of verifying your concept, performing market research, and producing a sound business plan. It will offer you the essential skills to develop your passion into a viable and sustainable enterprise.

No of your experience or degree of knowledge, this book will serve as your thorough guide, helping you to negotiate the complexity of business. By giving practical guidance, real-world examples, and tangible strategies, it attempts to encourage confidence, stimulate creativity, and equip you with the skills required to thrive in the fascinating world of entrepreneurship.

C. What to Expect from the Book:
A Roadmap to Entrepreneurial Success

As you begin on your business path, it's crucial to know what to anticipate from this book. Here's a preview of what is ahead and the helpful insights you may anticipate:

1. Comprehensive Coverage: This book covers all the fundamental components of beginning and operating your own company. From developing company ideas to establishing a business plan, from marketing and sales techniques to financial management and scaling, you'll discover a wealth of knowledge and practical guidance to aid you every step of the way.

2. Actionable advice: Each chapter is meant to give you actionable advice and practical measures to follow. You'll discover exercises, checklists, and case studies that will help you apply the ideas and principles directly to your business ventures. By actively interacting with the information, you'll be able to make progress and see concrete benefits.

3. Real-World instances: Throughout the book, you'll discover real-world instances of successful firms and entrepreneurs who have navigated comparable problems and achieved incredible achievements. These examples will act as inspiration and give vital insights into what it takes to develop a great company.

4. Expert Advice: As a professional in the business sector, I offer my skills and knowledge to this book. You can expect to gain from my knowledge and ideas, as I provide practical techniques, methods, and best practices that have been proven beneficial in the entrepreneurial world. I hope to equip you with the skills you need to make educated choices and conquer difficulties.

5. Holistic Approach: This book offers a holistic approach to entrepreneurship, understanding that success is not restricted to a single facet but depends on a mix of aspects. You'll get insights into marketing, sales, finance, operations, legal issues, and more. By understanding the interdependence of these factors, you'll be able to construct a firm foundation for your company.

6. Resources and References: To further help your business path, this book presents extra resources and references. You'll discover suggested books, websites, and resources that may enhance your study and give extra direction as you go.

By the conclusion of this book, you may expect to have a full awareness of the entrepreneurial environment, the skills required to succeed, and a plan to lead you through the obstacles and possibilities of beginning your firm. It will be a useful resource as you begin your journey and aim for long-term success.

CHAPTER 1
UNDERSTANDING
ENTREPRENEURSHIP

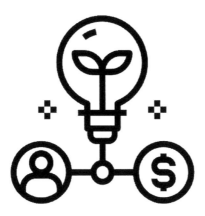

A. What is Entrepreneurship?

Unleashing the Spirit of Innovation and Opportunity

In this part, we will investigate the core notion of entrepreneurship and obtain a thorough knowledge of what it genuinely entails. Let's go into the meaning and substance of entrepreneurship:

Entrepreneurship may be characterized as the process of recognizing, generating, and pursuing chances to create, build, and manage a commercial endeavor. It requires the vision, ambition, and commitment to bring ideas into reality, typically in the face of uncertainty and danger. Entrepreneurs are people who exhibit a unique combination of attributes, including inventiveness, resilience, flexibility, and a dogged pursuit of their objectives.

At its root, entrepreneurship is about more than simply creating a firm. It symbolizes an attitude of searching out possibilities, taking prudent risks, and producing value in the marketplace. Entrepreneurs are motivated by a desire to solve problems, meet unmet needs, and have a good effect on society. They challenge the current quo, disrupt industries, and promote economic progress.

Entrepreneurship is not confined to any one sector, age group, or educational background. It is an attitude that can be adopted by anybody who has the desire, commitment, and willingness to take action. Whether you're founding a software firm, operating a small retail shop, or delivering unique services, entrepreneurship is about following your idea and bringing it to life.

B. Traits and Skills of Successful Entrepreneurs:
Unleashing Your Potential

In this part, we will analyze the qualities and talents that are typically seen among successful entrepreneurs. By knowing these attributes, you may find places to cultivate and strengthen within yourself as you begin on your business path. Let's look into the essential attributes and talents of successful entrepreneurs:

1. enthusiasm and Self-Motivation: Successful entrepreneurs are fueled by a genuine enthusiasm for what they do. They have a real excitement for their company concept or sector, which drives their devotion and determination. This enthusiasm acts as a tremendous motivator, helping people overcome challenges and remain focused on their objectives.
2. Resilience and Perseverance: Entrepreneurship is generally accompanied by failures and obstacles. Successful entrepreneurs possess a resilient attitude, enabling them to bounce back from disappointments, learn from their errors, and keep moving ahead. They can accept hardship, regard it as a chance for progress, and endure despite hurdles.
3. Visionary Thinking: Entrepreneurs can conceive possibilities and understand the wider picture. They can spot trends, foresee market movements, and picture the future of their firm. This visionary thinking

helps them to define strategic objectives, make educated judgments, and remain ahead of the competition.

4. Creativity and Innovation: Entrepreneurs are generally noted for their ability to think creatively and come up with novel ideas. They are not scared to question traditional thinking and seek fresh ideas. By thinking beyond the box, entrepreneurs may unearth innovative company ideas, distinguish themselves in the market, and drive innovation.

5. Risk-Taking and Measured Decision-Making: Successful entrepreneurs are comfortable with taking chances, but they do it in a measured way. They undertake comprehensive research, examine prospective consequences, and make educated judgments based on available facts. They recognize that entrepreneurship necessarily implies a degree of uncertainty and are prepared to take measured risks to attain their aims.

6. Strong Leadership and Communication: Entrepreneurs need to inspire and lead their staff successfully. They exhibit good leadership qualities, which include the ability to explain their vision, allocate duties, and encourage people. Effective communication assists entrepreneurs in creating connections, acquiring collaborations, and expressing their business's value proposition to clients and investors.

7. Adaptability and Flexibility: Entrepreneurship demands the ness to adjust to changing circumstances and manage developing market conditions. Successful entrepreneurs are adaptable and ready to modify their plans as required. They can swiftly pivot, grasp fresh possibilities, and overcome problems with agility.

8. Financial Management and Business Acumen: Entrepreneurs require a thorough grasp of financial management and business fundamentals. They can efficiently manage budgets, evaluate financial data, and make educated choices to maintain the financial health and development of their initiatives. company acumen helps them to spot industry trends, comprehend client wants, and establish viable company strategies.

9. Networking and Relationship Development: Entrepreneurs know the necessity of developing a strong network of connections. They actively participate in networking activities, attend industry events, and cultivate

contacts with future clients, partners, and mentors. Networking gives excellent chances for cooperation, mentoring, and company success.

10. Continuous Learning and Adaptation: Successful entrepreneurs have a passion for information and a dedication to continual learning. They keep current on industry developments, solicit input from customers and mentors, and actively seek chances for personal and professional improvement. By consistently learning and adjusting, entrepreneurs may remain ahead in their industry and create innovation.

While not every entrepreneur has all of these qualities and talents from the outset, they may be cultivated and perfected through time. By concentrating on fostering these attributes inside yourself, you may boost your chances of success as an entrepreneur.

C. Identifying Opportunities:
Unleashing Your Entrepreneurial Vision

In this part, we will discuss the process of discovering opportunities as an entrepreneur. Recognizing and capitalizing on opportunities is a fundamental talent that sets successful businesses unique. Let's look into the essential processes involved in recognizing opportunities:

1. Market Research: Conduct detailed market research to understand industry trends, client wants, and possible gaps in the market. Analyze market demographics, competitive information, and consumer behavior to uncover unmet requirements or underdeveloped markets. This study will give significant insights into prospective business prospects.

2. Problem Solving: Look for difficulties or pain spots that exist in the market or people's lives. Successful entrepreneurs typically develop inventive solutions to these difficulties, producing value and fulfilling consumers' requirements. By finding places where there is a desire for change or a better solution, you might unearth chances for entrepreneurial initiatives.

3. Observing Trends: Stay current on new trends, technology breakthroughs, and social transformations. These shifts might bring up

new chances for firms. By seeing and studying the changes occurring around you, you may uncover areas where your talents, expertise, or passion connect with developing trends, offering you a competitive advantage.

4. Leveraging Your Passion and Experience: Consider your hobbies, interests, and areas of experience. Reflect on what you like doing and the talents you have built through time. By matching your entrepreneurial activities with your passion and skills, you may utilize your particular assets and boost the probability of success.

5. Networking and Collaboration: Engage in networking activities and create contacts with persons in diverse sectors. Collaborating with others may lead to fresh insights, ideas, and cooperation possibilities. By broadening your network and participating in meaningful discussions, you may come across fresh possibilities or uncover possible partners who may complement your talents and resources.

6. Embracing Change and Innovation: Be open to change and welcome innovation. Markets and sectors are continually shifting, giving new chances for entrepreneurial initiatives. Stay adaptive and open to explore new ideas, technology, and business models. Embracing change helps you to remain ahead of the curve and embrace opportunities as they occur.

7. Feedback and Customer Insights: Seek input from prospective clients or target market sectors. Engage in talks, perform surveys, or collect data to understand their pain spots, needs, and preferences. By listening to your consumers and adopting their thoughts, you may uncover possibilities to produce goods or services that satisfy their requirements.

8. Analyzing Personal and Industry Challenges: Reflect on the obstacles you confront in your personal life or within your business. These obstacles may frequently be translated into commercial opportunities. By identifying frequent pain spots or inefficiencies, you may design new solutions that solve these difficulties and provide value for consumers.

Remember, recognizing possibilities needs a mix of curiosity, awareness, investigation, and imagination. By actively searching out chances and being open to new ideas, you may unearth hidden gems that have the potential to become great business endeavors.

D. Assessing Market Demand:

Navigating the Landscape of Customer Needs

In this part, we will go into the essential stage of gauging market demand for your possible company concept. Understanding the demands, tastes, and habits of your target market is vital for developing a successful organization. Let's review the essential factors for measuring market demand:

1. Target Market Identification: Identify your target market, which refers to the precise set of clients who are most likely to be interested in your product or service. Consider aspects like as demography, psychographics, and geographic location. By selecting your target market, you can concentrate your efforts on knowing their wants and preferences.

2. Customer Research: Conduct extensive customer research to get insights into their wants, preferences, pain areas, and habits. Utilize numerous research techniques, including surveys, interviews, focus groups, or observation. Collect data and analyze it to identify patterns and trends. This study will give useful information about market demand and help you modify your offers properly.

3. Competitive Analysis: Evaluate your rivals and examine their products, pricing, marketing techniques, and client base. Understanding the competitive environment helps you to find gaps or places where you can distinguish your firm. Assessing the strengths and weaknesses of your competition can help you position your goods or services successfully in the market.

4. Market Size and Growth Potential: Evaluate the size of your target market and analyze its growth potential. Consider aspects such as population size, buying power, and industry trends. Determine if the

market is big enough to maintain your firm and support its development. Identifying market sectors or niches with untapped potential may also create chances for differentiation and market entrance.

5. Trends and Market Shifts: Stay current on industry trends, technology breakthroughs, and changes in customer behavior. Assess how these trends may affect the demand for your product or service. By connecting your offers with rising trends, you may present your organization as innovative and fulfill shifting client wants.

6. price and Value Proposition: Evaluate how your target market sees the value of your product or service and select an acceptable price approach. Assess if clients are willing to pay for the advantages and solutions you provide. Understand the price dynamics within your sector and how your pricing compares to rivals.

7. Test and Validation: Consider doing small-scale testing or pilot projects to verify the demand for your product or service. This might entail selling a restricted version of your product, operating a beta program, or doing pre-orders. Collect input from early clients and utilize it to develop your service and marketing plan.

8. Iterative Approach: Recognize that gauging market demand is a constant activity. Stay alert to client input, adjust to changing market circumstances, and modify your offers depending on customer preferences. Regularly monitor and evaluate market trends and feedback to find chances for improvement or development.

By properly evaluating market demand, you may ensure that there is a viable consumer base for your company proposal. This insight will influence your strategic choices, marketing activities, and product development, eventually enhancing your chances of success.

CHAPTER 2

DEFINING YOUR BUSINESS IDEA

A. Generating Business Ideas:

Unleashing Your Entrepreneurial Creativity

In this part, we will study numerous strategies and tactics to produce company ideas. Coming up with new and profitable company ideas is an exciting and vital stage in beginning your firm. Let's go into the process of producing company ideas:

1. Identify Personal Interests and Passions: Reflect on your interests, hobbies, and passions. What hobbies do you enjoy? What subjects or industries fascinate you? Consider how you may harness your interests to generate a company concept that matches your passion. This method not only boosts your drive but also helps you to add unique thoughts and skills to your enterprise.

2. Problem-Solving and Needs-Based Approach: Look for issues or unmet needs in the market or people's lives. Pay attention to difficulties, inefficiencies, or problems that you or others confront. Think about how

you may build a solution to solve these difficulties and meet unmet requirements. This method helps you to generate value by giving solutions that make people's lives simpler, more efficient, or more pleasurable.

3. Industry and Market Research: Research diverse industries, markets, and trends. Explore new areas, technology developments, and changing consumer habits. Look for gaps or unexplored potential within these sectors. By remaining educated about market dynamics and industry trends, you may find areas where you can offer innovation and build a competitive edge.

4. SWOT study: Perform a SWOT (Strengths, Weaknesses, Opportunities, and Threats) study for distinct industries or market segments. Assess the internal and external elements that might affect a business's performance. Identify the assets and unique qualities you possess that may be used, as well as possible vulnerabilities or dangers that need to be addressed. Analyze the potential inside the market and how you may position yourself to capitalize on them.

5. Brainstorming and Idea Generation Techniques: Engage in brainstorming sessions, either independently or with a group of like-minded people. Use strategies like mind mapping, free association, or the SCAMPER approach (Substitute, Combine, Adapt, Modify, put to Another Use, Eliminate, Reverse) to develop a broad variety of ideas. Encourage creativity and explore alternative techniques to develop distinctive business concepts.

6. Discover market Gaps and Trends: Analyze current goods or services in the market and discover any gaps or opportunities for improvement. Pay attention to client comments, reviews, and ideas. Additionally, examine upcoming trends and developments in technology, sustainability, social responsibility, or other related areas. Combining current market gaps with rising trends might lead to novel company concepts.

7. Leveraging Your Talents and Expertise: Consider your unique talents, knowledge, and expertise. What are you extremely excellent at? How can you utilize your skills to generate value for others? Your

professional history, education, or unique skill sets might give a good basis for building a company concept in a specialized sector or industry.

8. Collaboration and Networking: Engage in dialogues and collaborations with other entrepreneurs, industry experts, or people from other backgrounds. Attend networking events, join entrepreneurial groups or online forums, and seek mentoring. Sharing thoughts and viewpoints with others may stimulate fresh insights and lead to the discovery of possible business ideas.

Remember, the process of producing business ideas is iterative and experimental. It demands an open mind, inventiveness, and a willingness to explore numerous routes. Be prepared to revise and iterate on your ideas as you receive feedback and further improve them. In the following part, we will study how to assess and modify your company's ideas to guarantee their feasibility and potential for success.

B. Evaluating the Feasibility of Your Idea:
From Concept to Reality

In this part, we will address the essential process of analyzing the viability of your company concept. Assessing the feasibility and possible success of your concept is vital before dedicating time, money, and effort to its execution. Let's review the important factors in analyzing your idea's feasibility:

1. Market study: Conduct a detailed market study to determine the demand, competition, and possible target market for your product or service. Identify the size of the market, growth potential, and any obstacles to entry. Evaluate the competitive environment and examine how your proposal varies from current options. This research will help you measure the market potential and the feasibility of your proposal.

2. Target Customer Validation: Validate your concept by getting input from your target customers. Conduct surveys, interviews, or focus groups to obtain insights on their needs, preferences, and willingness to pay for your service. Use their input to enhance your proposal and

discover any required modifications to satisfy their expectations. The validation process helps guarantee that your concept matches with client's wants.

3. Unique Value Proposition: Clearly describe your unique value proposition - the precise benefits and advantages your product or service delivers compared to rivals. Assess if your concept addresses an issue, answers a demand, or gives a unique edge in the market. Determine whether your value offer is strong enough to attract clients and stand out in a competitive field.

4. Financial study: Evaluate the financial viability of your plan by completing a complete study of the estimated expenses, income sources, and possible profitability. Estimate the initial costs, continuing expenditures, pricing strategies, and sales estimates. Consider aspects such as manufacturing costs, marketing charges, distribution networks, and possible scalability. This study will help you decide whether your concept has the potential for lasting financial success.

5. Resource Assessment: Assess the resources necessary to bring your concept to reality. Consider the people resources, skills, technology, infrastructure, and partnerships required to execute your company strategy. Determine whether you have access to or can obtain the required resources to execute and maintain your project. Identify any resource shortfalls and examine strategies for addressing them, such as recruiting, outsourcing, or partnering with strategic partners.

6. Legal and Regulatory Considerations: Investigate the legal and regulatory requirements involved with your company plan. Research licenses, permissions, certificates, and other industry-specific requirements that may apply. Ensure that you comply with all legal responsibilities and examine any possible legal or compliance concerns related to your proposal. Understanding the legal environment helps minimize future challenges and ensures your organization works within the limitations of the law.

7. Scalability and Growth Potential: Evaluate the scalability and growth potential of your concept. Consider whether your firm can grow and

manage rising demand over time. Assess whether there are chances for diversification, regional growth, or the introduction of new goods or services. A scalable company strategy provides for sustained development and enhanced profitability in the long run.

8. Risk Analysis: Conduct a detailed risk analysis to identify and analyze any risks and obstacles related to your project. Consider elements such as market risks, competitive risks, financial risks, operational risks, and external risks (e.g., economic, technical, or regulatory developments). Develop contingency plans and techniques to manage these risks and ensure your idea's durability in the face of obstacles.

By examining the viability of your project, you can make educated judgments and estimate the possibility of success before spending substantial resources. It is crucial to remain impartial and realistic throughout this assessment procedure.

C. Conducting Market Research:
Unveiling Insights for Informed Decision-Making

In this part, we will go into the process of performing market research to acquire vital insights for your company concept. Market research gives critical information about your target market, competition, and industry trends, helping you to make educated choices. Let's discuss the essential stages involved in performing market research:

1. Define study goals:

Clearly explain your study goals. Identify the precise facts you wish to obtain and the questions you want to answer. This might involve researching client preferences, determining market size, identifying rivals, or studying price dynamics. Defining your study goals ensures that your efforts are focused and targeted.

2. Primary Research:

Primary research entails acquiring fresh data directly from your target audience. There are numerous strategies you might employ:

a. Surveys: Create and run surveys to acquire quantitative data. Design questions that gather demographic information, preferences, buying habits, or input on your company concept. Surveys may be performed online, over email, or in person.
b. Interviews: Conduct one-on-one interviews with people from your target market to gather qualitative perspectives. In-depth interviews give a better insight into client motives, pain spots, and preferences. Use open-ended questions to promote thorough replies.
c. Focus Groups: Organize focus groups with a small number of persons that reflect your target market. Facilitate group talks to elicit ideas, foster engagement, and explore alternative views. Focus groups give essential qualitative data and enable for in-depth study of concepts.
3. Secondary Research:

Secondary research entails obtaining existing data and information from numerous sources. This might include:

a. Market Reports: Access industry reports, market studies, or published research to obtain insights into market trends, consumer behavior, and industry analysis. These studies contain essential data and may enrich your knowledge of the industry environment.
b. Competitor Analysis: Research your rivals to learn their goods, prices, marketing methods, and target audience. Analyze their strengths, shortcomings, and market positioning. This research helps you uncover areas of uniqueness and possible competitive advantages for your firm.
c. Online Sources: Utilize online platforms, social media, forums, and review sites to acquire information on client views, preferences, and trends. Monitor debates and attitudes about your industry, goods, or relevant subjects. Online sources give real-time data about consumer attitudes and behavior.
4. Data Analysis: Analyze the obtained data to uncover patterns, trends, and critical results. Use statistical analysis for quantitative data and

thematic analysis for qualitative data. Look for common themes, client preferences, and areas of potential. Data analysis helps you to make data-driven choices and find meaningful insights.

5. Competitive Benchmarking: Compare your company concept and products against rivals in the market. Assess their strengths, limitations, pricing methods, marketing approaches, and customer satisfaction levels. Benchmarking helps you to find areas where businesses may distinguish and get a competitive advantage.

6. Target Market Segmentation: Analyze the acquired data to discover unique segments within your target market. Segment your audience based on demographics, psychographics, behavior, or other relevant variables. This segmentation helps adapt your marketing strategy and services to certain consumer groups.

7. Interpretation and Application: Translate the study results into practical insights. Use the information acquired to improve your company concept, marketing strategy, product development, price choices, and customer acquisition techniques. Apply the information to make educated choices that correspond with consumer demands and preferences.

Remember, market research is a continuous activity that should be undertaken frequently to keep current on industry dynamics and growing client preferences. The insights acquired from market research give a strong platform for establishing a successful company strategy.

D. Identifying Your Target Market:
Finding Your Ideal Customer

In this part, we will explore the necessity of selecting your target market, a specific set of people who are most likely to be interested in your product or service. Understanding your target market helps you to adjust your marketing activities, language, and product offers to fit their requirements and preferences. Let's review the essential stages in selecting your target market:

1. Market Segmentation: Divide the wider market into separate groups based on common qualities, such as demographics, psychographics, behavior, or geographic location. This segmentation enables you to concentrate on distinct consumer groups with unique demands and preferences. Consider criteria like age, gender, income level, lifestyle, hobbies, values, and shopping habits.

2. Customer Profiling: Develop thorough profiles or personas of your target customers within each group. These profiles should contain information about their demographics, interests, motivations, difficulties, and objectives. Create a realistic image of your ideal consumer to drive your marketing efforts and product development.

3. Customer Research: Conduct primary research, such as surveys, interviews, or focus groups, to gain insights directly from your target market. Ask inquiries about their requirements, pain spots, preferences, and buying habits. Use the data acquired to confirm and enhance your knowledge of your target market and their unique needs.

4. Market Size and Potential: Assess the size and potential of each target market category. Consider aspects such as population size, growth patterns, buying power, and market saturation. Determine whether the sector is big enough to sustain your company and if it corresponds with your growth ambitions.

5. Competition Analysis: Analyze the competition within each target market category. Identify the important players, their products, prices, marketing methods, and consumer base. Assess the strengths and weaknesses of your competition to uncover areas where you may distinguish and give unique value to your target clients.

6. Customer Behavior and Trends: Stay updated about customer behavior and trends within your target market categories. Understand their interests, shopping patterns, online and offline activities, and outlets they utilize to get information. Monitor industry trends and changes in client preferences to predict developments in the market and alter your plans appropriately.

7. Problem-Solution Fit: Evaluate how effectively your product or service fits the unique demands and problems of your target market. Determine whether there is a clear problem-solution match, where your service delivers a compelling answer to a pain point or fits a particular demand. Aligning your product with the demands of your target market boosts its popularity and potential for success.

8. Iterative Refinement: Recognize that determining your target market is an iterative process. Continuously acquire feedback, evaluate data, and develop your knowledge of your clients. Adapt your methods as you learn more about their tastes, behavior, and changing market conditions.

By selecting your target market, you can concentrate your resources and efforts on reaching the appropriate people with the correct message. This tailored strategy optimizes your marketing efficacy, improves consumer engagement, and raises the possibility of conversion.

CHAPTER 3

CREATING A BUSINESS PLAN

A. Overview of a Business Plan:

Blueprint for Success

In this part, we will present an outline of a business plan, a thorough document that acts as a guide for your entrepreneurial path. A well-crafted business plan contains your company objectives, strategies, and operational details, helping you overcome the hurdles of beginning and sustaining a successful firm. Let's study the important components of a business plan:

1. Executive Summary: The executive summary is a succinct outline of your whole business strategy. It presents a picture of your firm, including its goal statement, core objectives, unique value proposition, target market, and financial highlights. Although it appears at the beginning of your plan, it is frequently written last, since it summarizes the major aspects of each component.

2. firm Description: This part offers a summary of your firm, its history, legal structure, and ownership. Describe your goods or services, target

market, competitive advantages, and important milestones attained. Highlight your objective, vision, and fundamental principles to provide readers with a clear idea of your firm.

3. Market study: Conduct a complete study of your target market, industry trends, and rivals. Provide an analysis of the market size, growth potential, and main market segments. Analyze your rivals' strengths and weaknesses, market positioning, and pricing tactics. Demonstrate your awareness of the market landscape and how your firm will prosper within it.

4. Organization and Management: Describe the structure and organization of your company. Identify important team members, their roles, responsibilities, and relevant experience. Outline your management team's credentials and skills. If relevant, add an organizational chart to explain the hierarchy and reporting structure.

5. Product or Service Line: Detail your items or services and their distinctive characteristics and advantages. Explain how they satisfy client demands and distinguish them from the competition. Discuss your product development lifecycle, intellectual property, and any proprietary technology or procedures. Include details about future product or service growth plans.

6. Marketing and Sales Strategy: Outline your marketing and sales tactics to attract and retain consumers. Define your target market segments and outline your positioning, branding, and price plans. Explain how you will reach your clients via advertising, promotions, digital marketing, and distribution networks. Include a sales projection and customer acquisition strategy.

7. Financial predictions: Present financial predictions, including income statements, balance sheets, and cash flow statements. Include predicted income, costs, and profitability for the following three to five years. Highlight significant assumptions and factors impacting your financial estimates. Provide a break-even analysis and describe your finance needs if seeking external financing.

8. Operations and Management: Explain how your firm will work on a day-to-day basis. Describe your operating procedures, production methodologies, quality control measures, and supply chain management. Discuss essential collaborations, suppliers, and resources necessary to supply your goods or services. Outline any operational issues you foresee and your mitigating methods.

9. Risk Assessment: Identify and analyze possible risks and difficulties that may influence your organization. This might include market risks, legislative changes, financial hazards, competitive challenges, or operational difficulties. Develop contingency plans and risk management methods to limit these hazards. Investors and stakeholders will appreciate your proactive approach to risk assessment and reduction.

10. Implementation Plan: Provide a clear timetable and action plan for establishing and expanding your firm. Break down your goals into concrete activities, assign responsibilities, and create milestones. Include key performance indicators (KPIs) to assess progress and quantify achievement. Demonstrate your capacity to implement your company ideas successfully.

Remember, a business plan is a living document that develops as your firm grows and changes. Regularly evaluate and revise your strategy to reflect new insights, market situations, and strategic developments. A well-prepared business plan not only acts as a guide for yourself but also demonstrates your professionalism and devotion to possible investors and partners.

B. Executive Summary:
Concise Overview of Your Business

The executive summary is a critical element of your business plan since it gives a succinct review of your whole strategy. It is often the first piece that readers will experience, and it should properly express the important components of your organization to attract their attention and interest. Let's discuss the fundamental components of an excellent executive summary:

1. firm Overview: Begin with a quick introduction to your firm. Summarize your company idea, its objective, and its vision. Clearly define the nature of your goods or services and the issue they address or the value they bring to clients. Provide an overview of your target market and the competition environment.

2. distinct Value Proposition: Highlight the distinct value your firm gives to consumers. Explain how your goods or services differ from rivals and why consumers would select you over other possibilities. Clearly describe your competitive advantages and the benefits consumers might anticipate by selecting your firm.

3. Market Opportunity: Present a persuasive argument for the market opportunity your organization seeks to exploit. Summarize the size and growth potential of your target market. Highlight any market trends or dynamics that generate beneficial circumstances for your firm. Showcase your grasp of the market and its potential for success.

4. company aims: Clearly describe your company's aims and ambitions. This might contain revenue objectives, market share ambitions, customer acquisition milestones, or growth strategies. Make your goals quantifiable and time-bound to establish a clear path for your firm.

5. Financial Summary: Provide a high-level review of your financial expectations. Highlight significant financial data, such as predicted revenue, profitability, and return on investment. Summarize any key expenses or investments necessary to establish or develop your firm. Showcase the potential for financial success and the desirability of your firm to prospective investors.

6. Management Team: Introduce the important members of your management team. Briefly summarize their relevant experience, abilities, and certifications. Highlight their abilities and their contributions to the success of your firm. Investors frequently pay great attention to the talents and track record of the management team.

7. support needs: If you are seeking external support, define your financial needs in this area. Indicate the amount of financing you are requesting and how you plan to utilize the cash. Explain how the investment will

help the development and profitability of your firm. Demonstrate the possible return on investment for prospective investors.

8. Call to Action: Conclude the executive summary with a call to action. Clearly express what you are seeking from the reader, whether it's a meeting, more conversation, or prospective investment. Provide contact information and invite interested persons to reach out for additional information.

Remember, the executive summary should be brief, interesting, and convincing. It should present a clear overview of your firm and create enough curiosity to inspire readers to look further into your business plan. Tailor the executive summary to your target audience, whether it's prospective investors, partners, or stakeholders.

After finishing the executive summary, it's advised to write it after the business plan preparation process. This helps you to correctly describe the essential ideas from each component of the strategy. Revise and revise the executive summary to ensure it properly communicates the substance of your business strategy and produces a great first impression.

C. Company Description:
Introducing Your Business

The company description part of your business plan gives an overview of your firm, its origins, structure, and significant features. It acts as an introduction to your firm and helps readers obtain a better idea of your company's identity and purpose. Let's review the crucial aspects to add to your business description:

1. firm description: Begin by introducing your firm and offering a quick description of its history, foundation, and present position. Include essential facts such as the date of creation, founders, and any major milestones or successes.
2. Mission and Vision: Clearly explain your company's mission, which outlines its basic purpose and reason for existing. Outline the beliefs and

concepts that govern your company choices. Additionally, describe your vision for the future, stressing your objectives and long-term goals.

3. Legal Form and Ownership: Specify the legal form of your organization, whether it's a sole proprietorship, partnership, limited liability company (LLC), or corporation. Describe the ownership structure and identify the major stakeholders or shareholders involved.

4. items or Services: Provide an outline of the items or services your organization provides. Explain the unique features, advantages, and value they bring to consumers. Highlight any competitive advantages or innovations that set your offerings distinct from those of rivals.

5. Target Market: Identify your target market and identify the client categories you plan to reach. Provide demographic information, such as age, gender, geography, income level, or other relevant qualities of your potential clients. This exhibits your grasp of your audience and their demands.

6. Competitive Advantage: Discuss your company's competitive advantages and what sets you different from the competition. This might include features such as unique knowledge, proprietary technology, exceptional customer service, cost benefits, or a distinct value offer. Clearly express why buyers would select your firm over alternatives.

7. Industry outline: Provide an outline of the industry in which your organization works. Discuss industry trends, growth forecasts, and any regulatory or market situations that may affect your firm. Show that you have a thorough knowledge of the industry environment and its prospects for success.

8. major accomplishments and Milestones: Highlight major accomplishments and milestones your organization has reached to date. This might be large revenue statistics, collaborations created, honors obtained, or successful product launches. Showcase your track record of achievement and show your ability to execute your company objectives.

9. Social Impact and Sustainability: If appropriate, outline any social impact or sustainability activities your organization promotes. Highlight

your devotion to ethical practices, corporate social responsibility, environmental sustainability, or community participation. This might increase your brand reputation and appeal to socially concerned shoppers.

10. Future ambitions: Briefly detail your company's future ambitions and growth strategy. Discuss any growth potential, new product or service innovations, or market expansion strategies. This displays your forward-thinking attitude and long-term vision for the organization.

The company description section should present a clear and appealing image of your organization, highlighting its distinctive traits, market positioning, and potential for success. It sets the setting for the remainder of your business plan and helps readers comprehend the environment in which your firm works.

D. Market Analysis:
Understanding Your Target Market

The market analysis portion of your business plan gives an in-depth insight into your target market, industry trends, client preferences, and competitive environment. It entails obtaining and evaluating relevant market data to inform your company's strategy and decision-making. Let's review the main components to include in your market analysis:

1. Industry Description: Begin by giving a complete description of the industry in which your organization works. Describe its size, growth rate, and major trends. Identify main companies, market segments, and any relevant regulatory or technical variables that impact the industry landscape. Showcase your awareness of the larger market context.

2. Target Market Segmentation: Identify and define your target market segments. Break down the bigger market into separate groups of clients who have comparable qualities, demands, and interests. Consider elements such as demographics (age, gender, income), psychographics (lifestyle, values), behavior (purchasing patterns, preferences), and

geographic location. This segmentation allows you to target your marketing efforts and services to certain client groups.

3. Customer Profile: Develop thorough customer profiles or personas for each target market category. Describe their features, goals, pain areas, and purchase habits. Consider aspects such as their requirements, preferences, goals, and obstacles. The more you understand your consumers, the more you can answer their demands and position your goods or services successfully.

4. Market Size and Growth: Determine the size and growth potential of your target market segments. Use available data, such as demographic statistics, industry reports, and market research, to determine the total addressable market (TAM) for your goods or services. Assess the growth patterns and estimates for your target market, demonstrating its potential for expansion and demand.

5. Market Trends and Opportunities: Identify and evaluate existing and developing trends within your target market and industry. This might include changes in consumer behavior, technical improvements, legislative upheavals, or cultural trends. Recognize possibilities that connect with your business's strengths and values, enabling you to capitalize on market trends and acquire a competitive advantage.

6. Competitive Analysis: Evaluate the competitive landscape within your industry. Identify direct and indirect rivals, their strengths and weaknesses, market positioning, pricing tactics, and unique selling propositions. Assess their market share and client base. Identify places where you may distinguish and deliver higher value to attract clients.

7. SWOT Analysis: Conduct a SWOT analysis (Strengths, Weaknesses, Opportunities, Threats) to examine your business's internal and external aspects. Identify your strengths and shortcomings, such as unique talents, resources, or operational efficiency. Recognize possibilities that you may capitalize on and possible risks that may hamper your progress. Use this analysis to design tactics that harness strengths and reduce weaknesses.

8. Customer Requirements and Preferences: Understand the requirements, preferences, and pain areas of your target customers. Gather data via surveys, interviews, focus groups, or market research to acquire insights into their purchasing habits, expectations, and satisfaction levels. This information lets you customize your goods, marketing messaging, and customer experiences to better satisfy their requirements.

9. hurdles to entrance: Identify any substantial hurdles to entrance in your target market. These might include significant beginning costs, regulatory restrictions, intellectual property problems, or severe rivalry. Assess how these hurdles may affect your company and establish methods to overcome or manage them successfully.

10. Market Entry Strategy: Outline your method of entering the market and obtaining clients. Describe your marketing and sales strategy, pricing models, distribution methods, and promotional activities. Consider how you will position your items or services to separate from the competition and attract your target clients.

A detailed market study reveals your extensive awareness of your target market, industry trends, and client preferences. It helps you discover opportunities, predict problems, and establish plans to successfully enter and flourish in the market. Use a mix of primary and secondary research approaches to acquire relevant data and assure its correctness.

E. Organizational Structure and Management:
Building an Effective Team

The organizational structure and management portion of your business plan defines the structure of your firm and introduces important members of your management team. It illustrates the organizational skills and knowledge essential to execute your company plan successfully. Let's review the main components to include in this section:

1. Organizational Structure: Describe the general structure of your organization. Identify the sort of organizational structure you have selected, such as a functional structure, divisional structure, or matrix

structure. Explain how various departments or teams are structured and how they communicate with each other. Provide an organizational chart to depict the hierarchy and reporting links.

2. Management Team: Introduce the important members of your management team and their duties. Include their professional backgrounds, credentials, and relevant experience. Highlight their expertise and how it matches the demands of your company. Convey why these people are well-suited to run your organization and contribute to its success.

3. Responsibilities and Roles: Outline the particular responsibilities and roles of each member of the management team. Clearly outline their areas of competence and authority. Discuss how these positions interact and work together to accomplish the company's objectives. This displays a clear separation of tasks and enables effective decision-making and implementation.

4. Advisory Board or Board of Directors: If appropriate, list any advisory board or board of director's members participating in your company. Highlight their skills and the value they provide to the firm via their counsel, industry knowledge, or network. This provides credibility and indicates that your organization has access to competent advisers or directors.

5. Personnel strategy: Provide a summary of your personnel strategy, which specifies the staffing needs of your organization. Discuss the estimated number of people required, their duties, and critical jobs that need to be filled. Highlight any unique skill sets or certifications necessary for certain roles. Discuss your approach to recruiting, training, and keeping exceptional staff.

6. Employee Compensation and Benefits: Briefly outline your approach to employee compensation and benefits. Highlight any competitive advantages or special incentives you give to recruit and retain outstanding employees. This might include competitive pay, performance-based incentives, health insurance, retirement programs, or professional development opportunities.

7. Management Succession Plan: Consider providing a management succession plan to indicate your preparation for future leadership changes. Discuss your strategy for creating and fostering internal talent for future management roles. This displays your dedication to long-term organizational stability and continuity.

8. essential External Resources: Identify any essential external resources or professional services you expect to engage in, such as legal advice, accounting services, or strategy advisors. Explain how these resources will assist your firm and contribute to its success. This indicates that you have addressed the requirement for external knowledge and have a strategy in place to obtain it.

9. Corporate Culture: Describe the intended corporate culture of your firm. Discuss the values, conventions, and principles that influence your company's operations. Explain how you propose to build a pleasant and inclusive work environment that encourages and engages people. A good company culture may recruit and retain top individuals and contribute to overall organizational success.

10. Human Resources Policies and Processes: Mention any key human resources policies and processes that you have created or intend to adopt. This might contain regulations about recruiting, training, performance assessment, employee behavior, and dispute resolution. Demonstrating that you have intelligent HR rules in place helps build a productive and pleasant work environment.

By displaying a well-defined organizational structure and management team, you create trust in investors, partners, and stakeholders. This portion of your business plan highlights the aggregate experience and talents of your team, guaranteeing that your organization is ready to implement its plans effectively.

F. Products and Services:

Offering Value to Customers

The goods and services part of your business plan contains the specifics of what your firm delivers to clients. It gives a complete explanation of your goods or services, stressing their features, advantages, and value proposition. Let's review the main components to include in this section:

1. Product or Service explanation: Begin by offering a clear and succinct explanation of your goods or services. Explain what they are, how they function, and what issues they address for clients. Provide explicit data about their features, functions, and any distinctive traits that separate them from rivals.

2. Value Proposition: Clearly describe the value proposition of your goods or services. Explain the primary benefits and advantages they give to consumers. Highlight how they answer client requirements, enhance their lives, or satisfy particular aspirations. Emphasize the value that buyers will gain from picking your solutions over alternatives.

3. Product/Service Development Stage: If your goods or services are still in development or have undergone recent upgrades, explain the current stage of development. Highlight any milestones accomplished and the strategy for future developments. This displays your dedication to ongoing development and keeping ahead of market trends.

4. Intellectual Property: If appropriate, explain any intellectual property linked with your goods or services. This might comprise patents, trademarks, copyrights, or trade secrets. Highlight how your intellectual property gives a competitive advantage and shields your ideas from being reproduced by rivals.

5. price plan: Outline your price plan for your goods or services. Explain how you have calculated the price structure, taking into mind elements such as manufacturing costs, market demand, competition, and perceived value. Justify your pricing approach based on your target market and your intended standing in the market.

6. Product/Service lifespan: Discuss the lifespan of your goods or services. Explain their present stage (e.g., introduction, growth, maturity, or decline) and how you intend to manage their lifetime efficiently. Discuss any initiatives for product/service extension, enhancements, or diversification to maintain continuous relevance and profitability.

7. Research and Development: Highlight any existing or planned research and development (R&D) initiatives connected to your goods or services. Discuss how R&D helps product/service innovation, differentiation, and market competitiveness. This indicates your dedication to keeping at the forefront of industry innovations.

8. production and Supply Chain: If appropriate, outline your production process or supply chain for providing your goods or services. Highlight any key alliances, suppliers, or manufacturing capabilities that add to the quality, efficiency, and dependability of your goods. Discuss any quality control techniques or certifications that maintain consistency and client satisfaction.

9. Product/Service plan: Provide a plan for future product or service offerings. Discuss your ideas for growing your product line, offering new features or versions, or branching into adjacent areas. This indicates your long-term vision and your capacity to react to shifting client wants and market conditions.

10. Customer Support and After-Sales Service: Describe the customer support and after-sales service you give to guarantee client satisfaction. Explain how you manage consumer inquiries, technical support, warranty claims, or product/service upgrades. Emphasize your dedication to offering outstanding client experiences throughout their journey with your firm.

By offering a clear and appealing explanation of your goods or services, you show your awareness of client demands and your ability to give value. This component of your business strategy helps investors, partners, and stakeholders acquire confidence in your services and their potential for success.

G. Marketing and Sales Strategy:
Reaching and Convincing Customers

The marketing and sales strategy portion of your business plan details how you will advertise and sell your goods or services to your target market. It outlines how you aim to raise awareness, attract leads, and convert them into paying clients. Let's review the main components to include in this section:

1. Target Market: Begin by reaffirming your target market and client groups. Provide a concise summary of the demographics, psychographics, and behavior of your target consumers. This guarantees that your marketing and sales activities are focused on the correct audience.

2. Marketing goals: Clearly describe your marketing goals. These might include developing brand recognition, gaining market share, expanding client base, or releasing new goods or services. Your goals should be clear, measurable, achievable, relevant, and time-bound (SMART) to lead your marketing activities efficiently.

3. Branding and Positioning: Explain how you will position your brand in the market and separate it from rivals. Discuss your brand identity, including your brand principles, personality, and visual aspects. Highlight the unique selling features (USPs) of your goods or services that set you apart and establish a strong brand image.

4. Marketing Channels: Identify the marketing channels you will utilize to reach your target market. This might comprise a mix of online and offline channels like as websites, social media, email marketing, search engine optimization (SEO), content marketing, advertising, events, public relations, and collaborations. Explain why these channels are ideal for your target audience and how you intend to use them successfully.

5. Marketing Campaigns: Outline particular marketing campaigns or activities you want to implement. Describe the primary messages, topics, and creative aspects that will be utilized to communicate with your target audience. Discuss the schedule, length, and intended consequences of each campaign. Include a budget allocation for each campaign to illustrate your financial preparation.

6. Sales Strategy: Describe your entire sales strategy and how you aim to create income. Discuss your sales method, whether it's direct sales, partnerships, distribution networks, or e-commerce. Outline your sales

process, including lead generation, qualifying, conversion, and post-sales support. Highlight any unique sales approaches or ideas that will provide you with a competitive edge.

7. Customer Acquisition: Explain how you will gain customers. Describe your lead-generating tactics, such as content marketing, advertising, social media campaigns, referrals, or strategic alliances. Discuss your method of turning leads into clients via tailored sales efforts, demos, trials, or incentives.

8. Customer Retention: Discuss your strategy for maintaining and nurturing current customers. Explain how you will promote consumer loyalty and drive repeat purchases. Outline customer retention techniques such as loyalty programs, tailored messages, post-sales assistance, and customer feedback tools. Emphasize the significance of providing outstanding client experiences.

9. price plan: Revisit your price plan and its connection with your marketing and sales initiatives. Discuss any special pricing, discounts, or bundling tactics you intend to employ to entice clients. Highlight the value proposition of your price and how it compares to rivals.

10. Marketing Budget: Provide a summary of your marketing budget. Discuss how much you intend to invest in various marketing initiatives and campaigns. Explain the logic behind your budget allocation and how you will measure the return on investment (ROI) for each marketing effort.

By presenting a well-defined marketing and sales plan, you show your expertise in how to approach and persuade your target clients successfully. This component of your business plan helps investors, partners, and stakeholders understand your strategy for increasing revenue and developing your client base.

H. Financial Projections:

Forecasting Your Business's Financial Performance

The financial projections portion of your business plan gives a thorough analysis of your company's predicted financial performance over a set time, often three to five years. It covers predictions for sales, costs, profit margins, cash flow, and important financial measures. Let's review the main components to include in this section:

1. Revenue Projections: Forecast your company's revenue by product/service category or client group. Use market research, historical data, industry trends, and sales predictions to anticipate future sales volumes and prices. Break out revenue predictions by month or quarter for the first year and then yearly for the succeeding years.

2. Cost of Goods Sold (COGS): Estimate the direct expenses involved with manufacturing or distributing your goods or services. Include expenditures such as raw materials, production charges, packaging, shipping, and any necessary royalties or licensing fees. Calculate the COGS as a proportion of sales to keep a clear picture of your profit margins.

3. running expenditures: Outline the projected running expenditures for your firm. This comprises expenditures such as rent, utilities, salaries, wages, marketing costs, professional fees, insurance, and administrative expenses. Categorize these charges and offer precise line items to guarantee thorough coverage.

4. Gross Margin and Operating Margin: Calculate the gross margin by deducting the COGS from the total revenue and expressing it as a percentage. This represents the profitability of each item sold. Additionally, compute the operational margin by deducting the operating expenditures from the gross margin and expressing it as a percentage. This gives insights into the profitability of your whole activities.

5. Cash Flow forecasts: Prepare cash flow forecasts to forecast the inflows and outflows of cash in your firm. This comprises funds from operating operations, investment activities, and financing activities. Project your cash flow on a monthly or quarterly basis to ensure you have adequate liquidity to satisfy your financial commitments and finance development plans.

6. Capital Expenditures: Identify any substantial capital expenditures your organization will spend, such as equipment purchases, facility renovations, or technology investments. Estimate the prices and timing of these expenditures and include them in your financial estimates. This indicates your awareness of the capital needs of your firm.

7. Break-Even Analysis: Conduct a break-even analysis to establish the amount of sales or income required to cover your fixed and variable expenses. This research helps you determine when your firm will become successful and gives insights into the scalability of your operations.

8. Financial Ratios: Calculate and evaluate important financial ratios such as return on investment (ROI), gross margin ratio, net profit margin, current ratio, and debt-to-equity ratio. These ratios give insights into the financial health and efficiency of your firm. Compare these ratios with industry benchmarks to gauge your company's success.

9. Sensitivity Analysis: Perform a sensitivity analysis to examine the effect of alternative scenarios or factors on your financial estimates. This helps you comprehend the various risks and uncertainties that may impact your business's financial performance.

10. money Requirements: If you need external money, clearly define your funding requirements and how the cash will be spent. Provide a breakdown of the finances required for launch expenditures, working capital, marketing campaigns, or any other specified goals. Outline your approach for repaying debts or giving a return on investment to investors.

By offering extensive and realistic financial predictions, you show your awareness of the financial feasibility and future profitability of your organization. This portion of your business plan lets investors and stakeholders analyze the financial attractiveness and sustainability of your enterprise.

I. Funding & Investment Options:
Financing Your Business Venture

The financing and investment choices part of your business plan gives an overview of the many sources of funds you may leverage to finance your organization. It details the finance needs, possible investors or lenders, and the terms and circumstances connected with each choice. Let's review the main components to include in this section:

1. financial needs: Start by clearly stating your financial needs. Estimate the entire capital required to establish and run your firm for a certain time, taking into consideration expenditures such as equipment, inventory, marketing, wages, and working capital. Break down the financing needs to offer a thorough picture of how the money will be distributed.

2. Personal Investment: Explain the amount of personal investment you are prepared to provide to the firm. This displays your devotion and confidence in the enterprise. Discuss any personal assets or savings you intend to employ and their estimated worth. Highlight how your commitment matches with the overall financial needs.

3. Debt Financing: Discuss the possibilities of acquiring debt financing from financial entities such as banks or credit unions. Outline the loan amount you are requesting, the repayment arrangements, and any collateral you may supply. Provide a summary of your creditworthiness and the actions you have taken to acquire favorable loan conditions.

4. Equity funding: Explore the prospect of getting equity funding from investors. Identify possible angel investors, venture capitalists, or private equity companies that may be interested in your sector or company proposal. Describe the investment amount you are seeking and the ownership percentage you are ready to provide in exchange. Explain how the funding will be employed to achieve company development.

5. crowdsourcing: Consider the possibilities of generating funds using crowdsourcing platforms. Explain how crowdsourcing works, including the many kinds (e.g., rewards-based, donation-based, equity-based) and platforms available. Discuss the advantages of crowdfunding, such as obtaining visibility, verifying your company concept, and accessing a wide pool of possible investors.

6. Government Grants and Subsidies: Research and find any government grants, subsidies, or incentives available for entrepreneurs in your sector or location. Provide information about the individual programs, eligibility requirements, and application procedure. Highlight how getting government money may help your business's financial requirements.

7. Strategic Partnerships: Explore the possibility of strategic partnerships or alliances with existing firms in your field. Discuss how these relationships may give financial assistance, access to resources, or distribution channels. Highlight any possible synergies and mutual advantages that may be obtained via such relationships.

8. Personal Networks: Consider utilizing your networks to get investments or loans. Discuss the potential of contacting relatives, family members, or acquaintances who may be interested in sponsoring your business effort. Highlight the terms and conditions connected with these agreements to guarantee openness and clarity.

9. finance schedule: Outline the schedule for acquiring finance and how it corresponds with your business's operating and development ambitions. Discuss any particular milestones or benchmarks you need to attain to entice investors or lenders. Provide a realistic timeframe that encompasses the due diligence process, discussions, and the time necessary to conclude financing transactions.

10. Financial predictions: Connect the financing and investment alternatives with your financial predictions. Show prospective investors or lenders how their funds will be employed and the estimated return on investment. Use the financial forecasts portion of your business plan to support your financing requests and illustrate the financial sustainability of your firm.

By delivering a detailed review of the finance and investment choices accessible to your organization, you show your awareness of the financial environment and your strategic approach to acquiring the required funds. This component of your business plan helps investors, lenders, and stakeholders assess the financial feasibility and appeal of your endeavor.

CHAPTER 4

LEGAL AND REGULATORY CONSIDERATIONS

A. Choosing a Business Structure:
Establishing the Right Legal Entity

Choosing the proper company structure is a crucial choice that will affect several areas of your organization, including legal liabilities, tax requirements, governance, and ownership. This part of your business plan gives an overview of the numerous company structures available and aids you in picking the most suited one. Let's discuss the important aspects of each structure:

1. Sole Proprietorship: A sole proprietorship is the simplest and most prevalent kind of company organization. It involves a single person owning and running the firm. As a single owner, you have entire

authority and responsibility for all elements of the firm. However, it also means you are personally accountable for any debts, liabilities, or legal responsibilities of the firm. This structure is excellent for small, low-risk firms with few personal assets at stake.

2. Partnership: A partnership is a company form where two or more persons share ownership and management duties. There are numerous forms of partnerships, including general partnerships and restricted partnerships. In a general partnership, all partners have equal duty and liability. In a limited partnership, some general partners take responsibility, and limited partners have limited liability but limited power. Partnerships enable shared decision-making, pooled financial resources, and perhaps increased knowledge. However, partners are jointly and individually accountable for the partnership's responsibilities.

3. Corporation: A corporation is a distinct legal entity from its owners, known as shareholders. It offers limited liability protection, meaning the owners' assets are typically safeguarded from the company's obligations. Corporations have a more sophisticated structure and need adherence to certain legal and regulatory standards. They may issue shares of stock and attract outside investors. Corporations are appropriate for firms wanting to acquire finance, have many owners, or operate in high-liability sectors.

4. Limited Liability Company (LLC): An LLC is a hybrid company form that contains aspects of both partnerships and corporations. It gives limited liability protection to its owners, known as members while giving freedom in administration and tax treatment. LLCs might have a single member or several members. This form is excellent for organizations that seek liability protection but want a simpler management structure compared to corporations.

When selecting a company structure, consider the following factors:

- responsibility: Assess the extent of personal responsibility you are prepared to undertake. Sole proprietorships and partnerships give less protection, whereas corporations and LLCs have limited liability.
- Ownership and Management: Determine how you want ownership and management to be organized. Partnerships include collaborative decision-making, whereas corporations and LLCs have specified ownership and management structures.
- Tax Considerations: Evaluate the tax consequences of each arrangement. Consider the effect on personal income tax, self-employment tax, and company tax. Consult with a tax professional to discover the unique tax benefits and drawbacks for your firm.
- Compliance and Regulation: Understand the legal and regulatory obligations connected with each structure. Consider the expenditures and administrative constraints associated with maintaining compliance with government rules, issuing yearly reports, and convening shareholder or member meetings.
- Future Growth and Finance: Assess your business's growth potential and finance requirements. If you want to seek external financing or go public in the future, a corporation may be more suited.

Consult with legal and financial specialists, such as lawyers and accountants, to fully grasp the ramifications and needs of each company structure. Selecting the correct structure is vital for providing a strong legal basis for your company and safeguarding your assets.

B. Registering Your Business Name:
Securing Your Identity and Brand

Registering your company name is a vital step in creating your identity and safeguarding your brand. This part of your business plan describes the process of registering your company name and the factors involved. Let's review the essential processes and elements to consider:

1. Choose a Unique Business Name: Select a unique and memorable name that expresses your business and connects with your target market.

Ensure that the selected name is not already in use by another firm in your sector or locality. Conduct a comprehensive search of existing company names, trademarks, and domain names to prevent possible conflicts or misunderstandings.

2. Legal Name vs. Trade Name: Understand the difference between your legal name and your trade name (also known as a "doing business as" or DBA name). Your legal name is the formal name of your company, registered with the proper government authorities. A trade name, on the other hand, is the moniker under which you do business and advertise your brand. In many countries, you may need to register your trade name separately from your legal name.

3. Check Availability: Search with the necessary government organizations, such as the Secretary of State or Companies Registrar, to check the availability of your selected company name. Many governments offer online databases or search tools to ease this procedure. If the name is available, you may continue with the registration procedure. If it's already in use, you will need to pick an alternative name.

4. Registration procedure: Follow the registration procedure indicated by the relevant government entity in your country. This may require completing registration paperwork, paying a registration fee, and presenting supporting papers. The particular rules and processes differ by area, so visit the official website or contact the local government for help. Some jurisdictions provide online registration alternatives for extra convenience.

5. Trademark Considerations: While registering your company name gives some kind of protection, it's equally vital to consider trademark registration. Trademarks give better legal protection and exclusive rights to use a certain name, logo, or phrase in connection with your products or services. Conduct a trademark check to guarantee your selected name does not infringe upon existing trademarks. Consult with a trademark attorney for help on the registration procedure and the amount of protection it gives.

6. Domain Name Registration: In today's digital world, getting a matching domain name is vital for creating an online presence. Once you have picked your company name, register a domain name that matches or closely corresponds to it. This helps develop consistency throughout your brand and makes it simpler for clients to locate you online. Register your domain name with a reliable domain registrar to assure its availability and ownership.

7. Brand Protection: Beyond registration, consider further actions to safeguard your brand, such as seeking for copyright protection for your logo or creative works, and developing procedures to monitor and handle any illegal use or infringement of your intellectual property. Consult with intellectual property professionals for thorough information on brand protection tactics.

By registering your company name and taking measures to protect your brand, you establish your firm's identity, increase brand awareness, and secure against possible conflicts or unlawful usage. This increases your standing in the industry and helps develop trust and confidence with your consumers.

C. Obtaining Necessary Licenses and Permits:
Compliance for Operating Your Business

Obtaining the proper licenses and permissions is a key step in assuring legal compliance and running your company in line with local, state, and federal requirements. This part of your business plan explains the process of finding and securing the appropriate licenses and permissions for your unique sector and area. Let's review the important concerns and processes involved:

1. Research Applicable Licenses and permissions: Begin by studying the licenses and permissions that are unique to your industry and locality. Different sectors have specific regulatory requirements, and the permissions you need will depend on the nature of your company's activity. Common licenses and permissions include basic business

licenses, professional licenses, health and safety permits, zoning permits, and environmental permits.

2. Identify Regulatory Agencies: Determine the regulatory agencies responsible for granting the licenses and permissions in your area. This may include municipal government entities, state departments, industry-specific boards or commissions, and federal agencies. Visit their websites or contact them directly to acquire information about the application procedure, needed documents, and related expenses.

3. Complete License and Permit Applications: Obtain the relevant application forms from the regulatory authorities. Fill out the forms carefully and include any needed supporting papers, such as proof of identification, evidence of company registration, financial statements, insurance certificates, or professional qualifications. Follow the directions supplied by the authorities and pay attention to any deadlines or other requirements.

4. Submit Applications and Pay Fees: Submit your completed license and permit applications to the various regulatory agencies. Ensure that you include all essential papers and payments as mentioned. Keep copies of your applications, receipts, and any communication for your records. Some agencies may provide online application submission alternatives for extra convenience.

5. Compliance Inspections: Depending on the nature of your company, you may be subject to inspections by regulatory bodies to verify compliance with health and safety standards, fire codes, zoning restrictions, or other special criteria. Prepare your business premises properly and solve any discovered faults swiftly to pass inspections successfully.

6. Ongoing Compliance and Renewals: Licenses and permits often have expiry dates and need frequent renewals. Stay aware of the renewal dates and commence the renewal procedure well in advance to prevent any gaps in compliance. Additionally, be aware of any changes in legislation or licensing requirements that may affect your firm and maintain continued compliance with relevant laws.

7. Industry-unique Considerations: Some businesses have unique licensing needs or certifications beyond standard business permissions. For example, enterprises in the food service sector may need food handling permits or liquor licenses, while healthcare practitioners need professional licenses or certificates. Research industry-specific rules and speak with industry groups or trade organizations for help.

8. Local Zoning and Permitting: Ensure that your company location is compatible with local zoning restrictions. Zoning regulations control how properties may be used for various purposes, and it's crucial to check that your company operations correspond with the zoning classification of your selected site. Obtain the appropriate zoning permissions or variances to operate lawfully.

9. Compliance help: If navigating the license and permitting procedure appears onerous, consider getting help from legal experts, business consultants, or industry-specific service providers who specialize in regulatory compliance. They can assist and guarantee you comprehend and complete all regulations.

By getting the proper licenses and permissions, you show your dedication to legal compliance, safeguard your firm from possible fines or closures, and create confidence with consumers and stakeholders. Compliance with regulatory regulations helps enhance your business's reputation and dependability.

D. Understanding Tax Obligations:

Navigating the Tax Landscape for Your Business

Understanding your tax responsibilities is vital for maintaining compliance with the tax rules and regulations of your country. This part of your business plan includes an outline of the important tax concerns and requirements you should be aware of as a company owner. Let's review the main factors of knowing tax obligations:

1. Tax Identification Number:

Obtain a tax identification number, such as an Employer Identification Number (EIN) or a Taxpayer Identification Number (TIN), depending on the regulations of your country. This number will be used to identify your firm for tax reasons and is important for submitting tax returns and other tax-related papers.

2. Business Tax forms:

Familiarize yourself with the many forms of taxes applied to companies. The particular taxes you are expected to pay will depend on criteria such as your company structure, location, and industry. Common forms of corporate taxes include:

- Income Tax: Businesses are normally liable to income tax on their earnings. The tax rates and filing procedures vary based on the company structure and tax legislation of your country.
- Employment Taxes: If you have workers, you will be responsible for withholding and remitting payroll taxes, such as Social Security, Medicare, and federal and state income tax withholdings. You may also be required to pay employer contributions for certain taxes.
- Sales Tax: If your firm sells products or services subject to sales tax, you need to collect and return sales tax to the proper tax authorities. Sales tax legislation and rates vary by jurisdiction, so ensure you grasp the requirements in your locale.
- Excise Tax: Excise taxes are charged on certain items or activities, such as gasoline, alcohol, cigarettes, or certain services. If your firm participates in activities subject to excise tax, investigate the appropriate rules and ensure compliance.
- Property Tax: Property tax is normally charged on real estate and personal property held by your firm. The tax rates and assessment techniques differ by jurisdiction.
- Other Taxes: Depending on your sector and area, there may be extra taxes or levies particular to your company. Examples include franchise taxes, company licensing taxes, or local taxes levied by municipal or county governments.

3. submitting and Payment Deadlines:

Be aware of the deadlines for submitting tax returns and making tax payments. These dates differ based on the kind of tax and the jurisdiction. Maintain a calendar or system to monitor crucial tax dates and guarantee timely compliance to avoid fines or interest costs.

4. Record-Keeping:

Maintain accurate and structured financial records to support your tax filings. Keep records of income, spending, receipts, invoices, and other important papers. This will expedite the preparation of tax returns, aid in justifying deductions or credits claimed, and offer proof in the case of an audit.

5. Tax Deductions and Credits:

Familiarize yourself with the tax deductions and credits available to companies. These may assist in minimizing your taxable income and lessen your total tax obligation. Common deductions include company expenditures, depreciation of assets, and payments to retirement programs. Research the precise deductions and credits applicable to your company and speak with a tax specialist for help.

6. Tax Professionals and Software:

Consider employing the services of a certified tax professional, such as an accountant or tax adviser, to aid with tax planning, preparation, and compliance. They may assist in ensuring you satisfy your tax requirements, uncover possible tax-saving possibilities, and give advice on complicated tax concerns. Alternatively, you may elect to utilize tax software particularly intended for companies to assist in easing the tax filing process.

7. Ongoing Tax Compliance:

Stay updated about changes in tax laws and regulations that may impact your firm. Tax rules are subject to modifications, and it is vital to remain current on any new requirements or incentives that might affect your tax responsibilities. Regularly assess your tax status and seek expert assistance as required to guarantee continuous compliance.

Understanding your tax duties and maintaining correct tax compliance is crucial for the financial health and security of your firm. By remaining educated, maintaining proper records, and getting expert help when required, you can navigate the tax environment successfully and reduce any tax-related risks.

E. Intellectual Property Protection:
Safeguarding Your Ideas and Innovations

Intellectual property (IP) protection is vital for firms that depend on unique ideas, technologies, or creative works. This part of your company strategy discusses the significance of intellectual property and gives an overview of the important issues for preserving your intellectual property assets. Let's discuss the numerous types of intellectual property and the methods you may take to secure them:

1. Types of Intellectual Property:

Intellectual property may be classed into numerous forms, including:

*   Copyright: Copyright protects original creative works, such as literary works, artistic creations, music, software code, and architectural designs. It gives exclusive rights to the creators, enabling them to control the reproduction, distribution, and public exhibition of their works.
*   Trademark: Trademarks protect unique signs, symbols, logos, names, or phrases that differentiate your goods or services from others in the marketplace. Registering a trademark gives legal protection and prohibits others from using identical marks that may create confusion among customers.
*   Patent: Patents protect innovations, methods, or innovative technical developments. They offer exclusive rights to the creator, forbidding anyone from creating, using, or selling the protected invention without

permission. Patents are normally issued for a set term, during which the creator may sell their idea.

- Trade Secret: Trade secrets refer to proprietary knowledge that gives a competitive advantage to your firm. This might comprise formulae, recipes, industrial procedures, customer lists, or marketing tactics. Protecting trade secrets requires keeping their confidentiality via procedures such as non-disclosure agreements (NDAs) and limited access to sensitive information.

- Industrial Design: Industrial design preserves the aesthetic or visual qualities of a product or thing. It encompasses the unique form, arrangement, pattern, or ornamentation that gives a thing its distinctive look.

2. discover and Evaluate Your Intellectual Property:

Examine your firm to discover the intellectual property assets you own. Determine which assets are most valuable and crucial to your company's success. This may include your brand name and trademark, proprietary technology or software, distinctive product designs, or copyrighted content. Evaluate the possible risks and advantages associated with each category of intellectual property.

3. Registration and Legal Protection:

Depending on the nature of intellectual property, registration with the relevant government authorities may be essential to guarantee legal protection. Consider the following steps:

- Copyright Registration: While copyright protection is inevitable with the production of original work, registering your copyright with the appropriate copyright office enhances your legal rights and gives proof of ownership in case of disputes.

- Trademark Registration: Registering your trademarks with the proper trademark office increases their protection and provides your exclusive rights to use them. Conduct a comprehensive check to verify your proposed trademark is not already registered or infringing upon current trademarks.

- Patent Registration: Patents need a formal application procedure, including thorough descriptions and specifications of the innovation. Consult with a patent attorney or agent to manage the difficult procedure and maximize the chances of successful patent registration.
- Trade Secret Protection: Implement internal rules and agreements to preserve your trade secrets. This might involve non-disclosure agreements (NDAs) with personnel, limited access to sensitive information, and encryption or digital security measures to preserve proprietary data.
- Industrial Design Registration: Depending on your location, you may be able to register your industrial designs to acquire legal protection against unlawful copying or imitation.

4. Monitor and Enforce Your Rights:

Regularly monitor the marketplace to discover any instances of possible infringement or unlawful use of your intellectual property. Take aggressive efforts to enforce your rights, such as writing stop and desist letters, commencing legal action, or finding alternate dispute resolution techniques.

5. Work with Intellectual Property Professionals:

Intellectual property concerns may be complicated, and getting help from intellectual property lawyers, agents, or consultants is recommended. These specialists can help you through the nuances of intellectual property law, assist with registration procedures, do IP searches and due diligence, and give advice on enforcing your rights.

6. International Considerations:

If your firm operates worldwide, remember that intellectual property rules and safeguards may differ between nations. Consider getting legal assistance to guarantee thorough protection of your intellectual property rights in each applicable jurisdiction.

Safeguarding your intellectual property assets is crucial for keeping your competitive edge and avoiding unlawful usage by others. By recognizing the numerous kinds of intellectual property, implementing appropriate registration and protection procedures, and actively monitoring and defending your rights, you may maximize the value of your intellectual property and reduce possible dangers.

CHAPTER 5

SETTING UP YOUR BUSINESS

A. Location Selection:

Choosing the Right Place for Your Business

Selecting the ideal location for your company is a key choice that may considerably affect its success. This part of your book advises on variables to consider when picking a place and offers insights into many aspects that might impact your selection. Let's review the important considerations of site selection for your business:

1. Target Market and Customer Accessibility: Consider the closeness of your selected site to your target market. Analyze demographic data, market research, and consumer profiles to identify where your potential customers are situated and how accessible your location will be to them. Factors to assess include population density, buying power, foot traffic, and transit infrastructure.

2. Competition and Market Presence: Assess the competitive environment in the region you are exploring. Evaluate the existence of comparable

firms and evaluate whether the market is saturated or if there is an opportunity for your company to flourish. Consider the positives and cons of being near rivals, such as the possibility of cooperation or higher exposure.

3. company Clusters and Networking Opportunities: Investigate whether there are company clusters or industry-specific hubs in the region. Being placed near comparable firms or inside an established industrial cluster might give networking possibilities, new alliances, and information exchange. It may also attract clients who are especially seeking items or services within that sector.

4. Infrastructure and Accessibility: Evaluate the infrastructure and accessibility of possible locales. Consider aspects such as closeness to transportation hubs (airports, seaports, highways), availability of parking or public transit, and simplicity of delivery logistics. Accessibility to suppliers, distributors, and other business partners is also vital to guarantee seamless operations.

5. Cost and Affordability: Assess the costs connected with the site, including rent or property acquisition rates, utilities, taxes, and maintenance fees. Consider your budget and compare it against the possible perks and advantages the place provides. Remember that cheaper sites may come with trade-offs in terms of market reach or company exposure.

6. Regulatory and Legal Considerations: Understand the regulatory and legal requirements particular to the selected area. This includes zoning rules, permits, licensing, and compliance with municipal, state, and federal laws. Ensure that your company operations correspond with the zoning rules and that you can satisfy any relevant regulatory duties.

7. facilities and Infrastructure Support: Take into consideration the availability of facilities and support services in the neighborhood. This includes access to banking facilities, business support groups, incubators or accelerators, networking possibilities, skilled labor pools, educational institutions, and healthcare facilities. These materials may help the development and sustainability of your firm.

8. Future development and Expansion: Anticipate your business's future demands and development possibilities. Consider whether the site can suit your growth objectives in terms of physical space, staff availability, and scalability. Assess the long-term sustainability of the site and if it corresponds with your company objectives.

9. Online Presence and E-Commerce Opportunities: In today's digital world, analyze the value of physical location vs online presence for your organization. Determine whether e-commerce skills can augment or perhaps replace the necessity for a conventional brick-and-mortar firm. Assess the possible advantages and costs associated with an online company strategy.

10. Personal Preferences and Lifestyle: Consider your personal preferences and lifestyle variables while picking a place. Assess the quality of life, community facilities, cultural offerings, and recreational activities in the region. A site that corresponds with your own beliefs and preferences might add to your overall happiness as a company owner.

By carefully examining these variables and completing sufficient research, you can make an educated choice when picking a site for your company. Remember that there is no one-size-fits-all solution, and the optimum location will depend on your sector, company model, and target market.

B. Setting Up a Home-Based Business:

Building Success from Your Home

Starting a home-based company provides flexibility, cost savings, and the option to work in a comfortable atmosphere. This part of your book assists in starting up and operating a successful home-based company. Let's review the major elements for creating and operating your company from home:

1. Legal and Regulatory Requirements: Research and understand the legal and regulatory requirements for establishing a home-based company in your location. Check zoning restrictions, homeowner association guidelines, and any permissions or licenses required for your unique

business activity. Ensure that your firm complies with all relevant laws to prevent any legal difficulties.

2. Dedicated workstation: Create a dedicated workstation inside your house that is distinct from your living quarters. This helps preserve attention, productivity, and a clear border between work and personal life. Designate a distinct room, corner, or office area where you may set up your equipment, keep supplies, and perform your company operations.

3. Equipment and Technology: Identify the essential equipment and technology needed for your home-based company. This may include computers, printers, internet access, phone lines, and any industry-specific equipment or gear. Ensure that you have dependable and efficient equipment to support your company operations.

4. Set Work Hours and Limits: Establish defined work hours and limits to ensure work-life balance. Determine when you will start and stop your work and express these limits to family members or roommates. Setting clear expectations helps develop a routine and reduces distractions during working hours.

5. company Image and Communication: Present a professional image for your home-based company. Create a separate business phone line or employ a professional phone answering service. Develop a professional email account and website to increase your internet visibility. Use excellent branding, logos, and marketing materials to build a reputation and attract consumers.

6. Time Management and Productivity: Develop efficient time management tactics to increase productivity. Set daily or weekly objectives, prioritize activities, and develop a plan that allows for concentrated work. Minimize distractions by establishing boundaries with family members, shutting off personal alerts, and maintaining a quiet and orderly workstation.

7. Client Meetings and Impressions: Consider how you will manage client meetings and impressions while working from home. Evaluate if you will meet customers in your home office, hire meeting venues, or opt

for virtual meetings. Ensure that your home office appears appealing and professional if customers or business partners come.

8. Communication and Collaboration Tools: Utilize communication and collaboration tools to remain connected with clients, customers, and team members. Explore choices like video conferencing, project management software, cloud storage, and instant messaging systems. These technologies promote seamless communication and cooperation regardless of your physical location.

9. Home company Insurance: Evaluate if you need extra insurance coverage for your home-based company. Homeowner's insurance may not offer enough protection for business-related obligations or assets. Consult with an insurance specialist to discover the proper coverage alternatives for your company.

10. Networking and assistance: Engage in networking activities and seek assistance from other home-based company owners or entrepreneurial groups. Join industry organizations, attend local business events, and engage in online forums or social media groups. Connecting with like-minded folks gives useful insights, support, and prospective business prospects.

11. Growth and Scalability: Consider the possibility of growth and scalability in your home-based company. Assess whether your existing arrangement can allow future development or if you may need to investigate alternate choices, such as renting extra space or transferring to a commercial site.

Running a successful home-based company involves discipline, organization, and good time management. By applying these tactics and keeping a professional mentality, you may develop a profitable company while enjoying the perks of working from home.

C. Acquiring Equipment and Supplies:
Equipping Your Business for Success

Acquiring the essential equipment and supplies is a critical step in establishing your company. This part of your book highlights the important factors for getting the correct equipment and supplies to support your company's operations. Let's discuss the procedures involved in getting the needed tools and resources for your business:

1. Identify Equipment and Supply Needs: Begin by determining the exact equipment and materials necessary for your firm. Consider the type of your firm, the services or goods you provide, and the operational activities involved. Make a complete inventory of all the products you will need to efficiently manage your firm.

2. Determine Equipment Budget: Set a budget for obtaining equipment and supplies. Research the market to acquire a sense of the approximate prices connected with the things on your list. Consider both the initial expenditures and any recurrent expenses like maintenance, upgrades, or consumables.

3. Research Equipment and Supplier Options: Conduct comprehensive research to discover reliable equipment suppliers or vendors. Compare pricing, quality, warranties, and user reviews. Seek advice from industry peers or connect with specialists who can give insights into the finest equipment solutions for your unique company requirements.

4. Consider New vs. old Equipment: Determine whether you will acquire new or old equipment. New equipment frequently comes with guarantees, the newest features, and longer lifespans, but it might be costlier. Used equipment may provide cost savings, but it's necessary to analyze its quality, dependability, and any possible repair or maintenance needs.

5. Financing alternatives: Explore numerous financing alternatives accessible to you. These may include standard bank loans, equipment leasing or financing schemes, or crowdsourcing sites. Consider the financial consequences of each choice, including interest rates, payback periods, and possible effects on your cash flow.

6. Test and Evaluate Equipment: Before completing any equipment purchases, if practical, test the equipment or request demonstrations to confirm it fulfills your needs. Evaluate criteria such as performance,

functionality, simplicity of use, and compatibility with your current systems or procedures.

7. Supplier ties and Service Agreements: Establish solid ties with your equipment suppliers or vendors. Consider variables such as delivery delays, after-sales assistance, warranty coverage, and repair services. Read and understand the terms and conditions of any service agreements to ensure you obtain quick support and avoid interruptions to your company operations.

8. Inventory & Supply Chain Management: Develop an efficient inventory management plan to guarantee you have an appropriate supply of important commodities. Implement systems to manage inventory levels, reorder points, and supplier connections. Consider issues like lead times, storage space needs, and cost efficiencies in managing your inventory.

9. Safety and Maintenance: Prioritize safety issues while obtaining equipment. Ensure that the equipment satisfies safety requirements and is properly maintained. Develop maintenance plans and processes to maintain your equipment in peak condition, lengthen its lifetime, and limit the chance of accidents or malfunctions.

10. Sustainable and Eco-Friendly Choices: Consider ecologically friendly solutions when obtaining equipment and supplies. Look for energy-efficient equipment, recyclable packaging, or sustainable materials. By emphasizing sustainability, you may contribute to environmental protection and strengthen your business's image as a responsible company.

11. Training and User Manuals: Provide enough training for yourself and your workers on the correct usage, maintenance, and safety practices related to the purchased equipment. Utilize user manuals, internet resources, or training courses given by equipment makers or providers. Well-trained workers can maximize equipment performance and limit the risk of accidents or abuse.

By carefully assessing your equipment and supply requirements, budgeting efficiently, and completing comprehensive research, you may purchase the required tools and resources to support your company operations. Remember to consider quality, usefulness, and long-term value while making equipment buying selections.

D. Building a Professional Team:
Assembling a Strong and Capable Workforce

Building a competent workforce is vital for the success and development of your organization. This part of your book discusses the important procedures and factors for constructing a strong and skilled team. Let's examine the process of developing a professional staff for your business:

1. Define Your Team Needs: Start by precisely outlining the roles and responsibilities you need to fill in your organization. Consider the exact skills, credentials, and experience necessary for each post. Determine the number of team members required and if they will be full-time, part-time, or contractors.
2. Develop Job Descriptions: Create complete job descriptions for each position you are recruiting for. Clearly explain the tasks, qualifications, and expectations for the job. Include desired abilities, educational background, relevant experience, and any special certifications or licenses necessary.
3. Attracting Talent: Develop a recruitment plan to attract competent individuals. Advertise job opportunities using numerous methods, such as online job boards, professional networks, industry-specific platforms, and social media. Craft appealing job posts that showcase the unique qualities of your firm and the possibilities it provides.
4. Screening and Interviewing applicants: Screen resumes and applications to identify applicants who satisfy the basic criteria. Conduct interviews to analyze individuals' credentials, abilities, and cultural fit. Use a blend of behavioral, situational, and competency-based interview questions to assess their skills and potential value to your firm.
5. Skills Assessment and Reference Checks: Assess applicants' skills and abilities using practical exams, work samples, or simulations, depending on the nature of the position. Verify their credentials and professional

experience by doing reference checks with their prior employers or trustworthy persons who may give insights into their work ethic and performance.

6. Cultural Fit and Values Alignment: Consider cultural fit and values alignment while assessing applicants. Assess if they connect with your business's purpose, vision, and fundamental values. A team that shares similar values and beliefs is more likely to cooperate well and work towards a shared objective.

7. remuneration and Benefits: Develop competitive remuneration packages based on industry norms, the individual function, and the amount of expertise necessary. Consider additional advantages and incentives, such as healthcare coverage, retirement plans, bonuses, professional development opportunities, and flexible work arrangements. Ensure that the remuneration and perks line with your budget and company objectives.

8. Onboarding and Training: Once you have picked qualified people, design an onboarding procedure to incorporate them into your organization seamlessly. Provide appropriate training, orientation, and advice to acquaint new personnel with your company operations, rules, processes, and expectations. This enables individuals to swiftly adjust to their duties and become effective members of the team.

9. Communication and cooperation: Foster effective communication and cooperation among your team. Establish clear routes of communication, encourage open debate, and cultivate a culture of openness and constructive criticism. Utilize communication tools, project management software, and frequent team meetings to promote cooperation and productivity.

10. Performance Assessment and Development: Implement performance assessment mechanisms to analyze individual and team performance. Set explicit objectives and expectations, offer frequent feedback, and celebrate successes. Offer chances for professional development and skill upgrading to support the growth and progress of your team members.

11. Retention ways: Develop ways to retain excellent employees inside your firm. Create a healthy work atmosphere, give possibilities for professional progression, and build a culture of respect and acknowledgment. Offer competitive wages, benefits, and work-life balance efforts to enhance employee happiness and loyalty.

Building a competent team needs careful planning, meticulous recruiting efforts, and continuing support and growth. By hiring the proper personnel who connect with your firm's aims and values, and establishing a collaborative and supportive work environment, you can develop a strong team that contributes to the success of your business.

E. Establishing a Web Presence:
Building Your Online Identity

In today's digital world, creating a strong online presence is vital for the success of your organization. This part of your book gives help in developing and maintaining your online persona. Let's review the important measures to develop a captivating online presence for your business:

1. Registering a Domain Name: Start by registering a domain name that represents your company name or brand. Choose a domain name that is memorable, topical, and simple to spell. Research domain registrars and choose a trusted service to obtain your preferred domain name.
2. Website Development: Develop a professional and user-friendly website to represent your company online. Consider the goal of your website (e.g., informative, e-commerce), your target audience, and your branding. Hire a web developer or use website builders and content management systems (CMS) to establish an aesthetically attractive and effective website.
3. Website Design and User Experience: Pay attention to website design features such as layout, color scheme, typography, and graphics. Ensure that your website is aesthetically attractive, simple to use, and suited for mobile devices. Aim to deliver a great user experience that engages and keeps visitors.

4. Compelling material: Create high-quality and relevant material for your website. Include useful and entertaining information, photographs, videos, and other assets that demonstrate your goods, services, or expertise. Develop a content strategy that connects with your company objectives and resonates with your target audience.

5. Search Engine Optimization (SEO): Implement SEO tactics to boost your website's visibility in search engine results. Conduct keyword research, optimize meta tags and descriptions, generate original and useful content, and establish excellent backlinks. SEO helps deliver organic traffic to your website and boosts your online visibility.

6. Social Media Presence: Establish a presence on key social media sites to engage with your target audience and promote your brand. Identify the sites where your audience is most engaged and establish compelling accounts. Regularly share material, communicate with fans, and leverage social media advertising to extend your reach.

7. Online Reputation Management: Monitor and manage your online reputation to preserve a favorable picture. Respond swiftly to consumer reviews, comments, and feedback, whether good or negative. Encourage pleased customers to submit reviews and testimonials, and resolve any concerns or problems mentioned by disgruntled consumers.

8. E-commerce Functionality: If you provide items or services for online purchase, consider incorporating e-commerce functionality on your website. Integrate secure payment channels, give thorough product information, and provide a seamless checkout experience. Ensure that your e-commerce platform is stable, user-friendly, and secure.

9. Regular Website Maintenance: Regularly update and maintain your website to guarantee its best functioning. Check for broken links, update material, and apply security fixes and updates. Regularly back up your website to avoid data loss and have a strategy in place to manage any technical difficulties that may emerge.

10. Analytics & Performance Tracking: Utilize web analytics tools to monitor and evaluate your website's performance. Monitor critical indicators such as website traffic, user behavior, conversion rates, and

engagement levels. Use these insights to create data-driven choices and consistently enhance your online presence.

11. Online Advertising and Marketing: Consider online advertising choices such as search engine marketing (SEM), display advertisements, social media ads, and influencer partnerships. Develop a digital marketing plan that corresponds with your company objectives and target audience. Monitor and adjust your internet advertising efforts to enhance their performance.

Establishing a successful online presence needs careful planning, attention to detail, and regular upkeep. By developing a professional website, optimizing it for search engines, connecting with your audience on social media, and other online marketing tactics, you can successfully promote your brand to a broader online audience.

CHAPTER 6

FINANCING YOUR BUSINESS

A. Self-funding Options:

Funding Your Business from Personal Resources

When beginning your own company, self-funding is one of the key strategies to finance your endeavor. This part of your book discusses several self-funding solutions that enable you to leverage your resources to support your company. Let's look into the many self-funding methods accessible to entrepreneurs:

1. own resources: Utilize your resources as a key source of financing for your company. This requires devoting a part of your amassed funds or liquidating assets to invest in your enterprise. Evaluate your financial status and evaluate how much cash you are willing to commit to your firm.

2. Retirement money: If you have a retirement account such as a 401(k) or Individual Retirement Account (IRA), you may consider utilizing a part of that money to finance your company. Options such as a Rollover for

firm Startups (ROBS) enable you to put retirement assets into your firm without experiencing early withdrawal fines or tax ramifications.

3. Home Equity: If you possess a property with equity, you may investigate alternatives like a home equity loan or line of credit to get funding for your company. This enables you to leverage the value of your house to acquire a loan with attractive interest rates and payback conditions.

4. Personal Loans: Consider asking for a personal loan from a bank, credit union, or internet lender to support your company. Personal loans are often unsecured and depend on your creditworthiness. Ensure that you thoroughly analyze the interest rates, payback conditions, and any related costs before continuing with a personal loan.

5. Credit Cards: Use personal or business credit cards to pay early starting fees and continuing expenditures. However, use caution when depending on credit cards, since high interest rates may rapidly amass debt. It's good to have a repayment plan in place and examine credit card alternatives with low introductory rates or rewards programs that might benefit your company.

6. Friends and Family: Approach friends and family members who may be interested in helping your company financially. Present a clear business strategy, define the risks and benefits, and establish the relationship with adequate legal papers. It's crucial to retain openness and straightforward communication to sustain personal connections.

7. Bootstrapping: Adopt a bootstrapping approach, where you value thrift and resourcefulness to support your firm. Cut wasteful spending, negotiate advantageous terms with suppliers, and enhance income generation. Bootstrapping enables you to keep complete ownership and control of your firm but may need patience and careful financial management.

8. Side Jobs or Freelancing: Take on side jobs or freelance work to earn extra revenue that may be invested in your firm. This permits you to retain a constant income flow while developing your business

enterprise. Allocate the revenues from these efforts towards supporting your firm.

9. Crowdfunding: Explore crowdfunding sites where people or organizations may donate cash to support your company's concept. Create an enticing campaign that effectively explains the value of your company and gives prizes or incentives to supporters. Crowdfunding not only offers financial assistance but also helps build first-market interest and validation.

10. Contest and Grant Opportunities: Participate in business competitions or apply for funds particularly geared to encourage businesses. These initiatives give cash assistance and typically provide mentoring or networking advantages. Research and locate appropriate competitions and grants that match your company's industry or population.

Remember to thoroughly examine your financial condition, consider the risks involved, and build a realistic budget and financial strategy for your firm. It's vital to create a balance between employing personal resources and protecting your financial security. Additionally, get help from financial specialists or business advisers to make educated judgments about self-funding possibilities.

B. Seeking Loans and Grants:

Exploring External Funding Sources

In addition to self-financing, entrepreneurs have the option to seek external capital via loans and grants. This part of your book explores the many loan and grant possibilities available to help your firm financially. Let's examine these external financing sources:

1. Small Business Administration (SBA) Loans: The U.S. Small Business Administration provides several lending programs aimed at helping small companies. The most common is the SBA 7(a) loan program, which offers finance for startups and established enterprises. SBA loans frequently offer advantageous interest rates and longer payback durations compared to conventional loans.

2. Bank financing: Approach conventional banks and financial organizations to enquire about company financing. Banks may provide term loans, lines of credit, or equipment financing alternatives. Prepare a detailed business plan, financial predictions, and documents confirming your company's sustainability to boost your chances of receiving a bank loan.

3. Microloans: Microloans are modest loans made by nonprofit organizations, community development financial institutions (CDFIs), and internet lenders. These loans are appropriate for enterprises with small financial requirements and are frequently more accessible to entrepreneurs with a short credit history or lower credit ratings.

4. Peer-to-Peer (P2P) Lending: P2P lending services link borrowers directly with individual investors who are prepared to lend money. These internet platforms promote borrowing at competitive interest rates, especially for persons with strong credit. Conduct comprehensive research and compare terms and rates before participating in P2P lending.

5. Angel Investors: Angel investors are people or organizations that invest their cash in potential firms in return for an ownership share. Seek out angel investor networks, attend pitch events, or exploit internet platforms to connect with possible investors. Prepare a captivating pitch deck and be ready to illustrate the possible returns on investment for your firm.

6. Venture Capital: Venture capital companies invest in high-growth enterprises with the potential for big rewards. These companies often seek enterprises in technology, innovation, and scalable sectors. Secure venture funding by demonstrating a sound company strategy, a strong team, and a clear route to profitability and development.

7. funds: Research funds granted by government agencies, private foundations, and nonprofit organizations. Grants give non-repayable cash to assist particular corporate operations, research and development, innovation, or community-focused projects. Explore grants that fit with your company's industry, demographics, or social impact objectives.

8. crowdsourcing: In addition to self-financing, crowdsourcing may act as a tool to seek external funds. Crowdfunding systems allow you to generate cash from a broad pool of people who donate lesser sums. Create an entertaining campaign, properly convey your company concept, and provide attractive prizes to attract supporters.

9. Business Incubators and Accelerators: Join business incubators or accelerators that give not just cash but also mentoring, resources, and networking opportunities. These programs frequently have a competitive application procedure, and successful candidates get cash assistance and advice to fast-track their company development.

10. Government Programs and Economic Development Initiatives: Investigate government programs and economic development projects at the municipal, regional, and national levels. These programs may give grants, low-interest loans, tax incentives, or other types of financial aid to stimulate entrepreneurship and economic development.

When pursuing loans and grants, ensure you have a good business plan, financial predictions, and evidence that indicate your firm's potential. Prepare a convincing pitch or grant proposal that effectively explains your vision, market opportunity, and value offer.

Remember to thoroughly analyze the terms and conditions of any external financing sources and consider the possible influence on your business's ownership and decision-making. Consult with financial consultants or business mentors to make educated judgments regarding the best financing possibilities for your firm.

C. Attracting Investors:

Securing Investment for Your Business

Attracting investors is a potential alternative for funding your company and having access to funds for development and expansion. This portion of your book dives into the techniques and factors involved in obtaining investors. Let's review the important measures to attract possible investors to your business:

1. Develop a Compelling Business Plan: Create a detailed business plan that details your company model, market analysis, competitive advantage, growth strategy, and financial predictions. Your business plan should clearly describe your goal, establish the potential for profitability, and emphasize the distinctive elements of your firm that make it interesting to investors.

2. Build a Strong Management Team: Investors are generally attracted to organizations run by skilled and experienced management teams. Surround yourself with skilled persons who compliment your abilities and help the overall success of the enterprise. Emphasize the skills and track record of your team members while pitching potential investors.

3. Identify Your Target Investors: Define your ideal investor profile based on their industry knowledge, investment preferences, and past investment track record. Research venture capital companies, angel investor networks, and other investment groups to uncover possible investors who correspond with your company area and development stage.

4. Craft an Effective Pitch Deck: Develop a short and effective pitch deck that emphasizes the essential components of your company and investment opportunity. Include details about your market, company model, competitive advantage, financial predictions, and exit plan. Keep the pitch deck aesthetically attractive, simple to grasp, and suited to the interests of your target investors.

5. Network and Attend Industry Events: Actively network within your sector and engage in relevant conferences, seminars, and startup activities. Attend pitch contests, demo days, and investor matchmaking events to exhibit your firm and meet with possible investors. Leverage your network to seek introductions to investors and establish a reputation via recommendations.

6. Engage in Due Diligence: Investors do extensive due diligence before making investing selections. Be prepared to give extra information, financial statements, legal papers, and any other needed items to assist

their review process. Anticipate and resolve possible issues or dangers that investors may have during due diligence.

7. Highlight Market Traction and Milestones: Demonstrate success and traction within your market to create trust in possible investors. Highlight major milestones, customer acquisition data, revenue growth, collaborations, or industry recognition that demonstrate your business's potential and separate it from rivals.

8. Seek Strategic alliances: Forge strategic alliances with industry leaders or adjacent firms that may provide significant value to your enterprise. Strategic relationships may give access to resources, distribution channels, experience, and prospective investor introductions. Highlight these ties as a strategic benefit during investor conversations.

9. Be Transparent and Communicate Effectively: Transparency and excellent communication are crucial when working with investors. Provide clear and accurate information, swiftly reply to queries, and show your dedication to open and honest communication. Establish trust and credibility by keeping investors informed about the development and issues of your firm.

10. Negotiate conditions and Structure: When investor interest is clear, embark into talks about investment conditions, equity ownership, value, and other pertinent considerations. Seek legal and financial assistance to ensure you understand the ramifications of the conditions being provided and negotiate for a fair and mutually profitable deal.

Remember that obtaining investors may be a time-consuming process, requiring perseverance and tenacity. Rejections are normal, so utilize feedback to better your pitch and approach. Every meeting with investors is a chance to learn and enhance your pitch for future interactions.

D. Crowdfunding and Alternative Financing Methods:
Exploring Innovative Funding Options

Crowdfunding and other finance techniques have gained popularity as viable means to obtain funds for enterprises. This portion of your book discusses the numerous choices open to entrepreneurs, including crowdfunding sites and other novel financing approaches. Let's delve into these alternate financing avenues:

1. Crowdfunding Platforms:

Crowdfunding platforms enable businesses to obtain capital from a large number of people who donate lesser sums. There are many forms of crowdfunding:

a. Awards-Based Crowdfunding: This sort of crowdfunding includes giving awards or incentives to supporters who donate cash to your campaign. These prizes might vary from early access to your product or service to special items or experiences. Popular rewards-based crowdfunding sites include Kickstarter and Indiegogo.

b. Equity-Based Crowdfunding: Equity-based crowdfunding enables you to raise funds by providing investors equity or shares in your firm. Platforms such as Seed Invest and Start Engine allow firms to connect with prospective investors and acquire funding in return for ownership holdings.

c. Donation-Based Crowdfunding: Donation-based crowdfunding entails gathering money from those who support your cause or business concept without expecting any financial rewards. This sort of crowdfunding is typically employed by social entrepreneurs, non-profit organizations, or initiatives with a charitable bent. Platforms like GoFundMe and Patreon enable donation-based crowdfunding.

2. Peer-to-Peer Lending:

Peer-to-peer (P2P) lending platforms link borrowers with independent lenders who are prepared to make loans. These internet platforms take out conventional financial middlemen and provide more flexible loan possibilities. P2P lending generally helps borrowers with less credit history or worse credit ratings to get finance. Popular P2P lending platforms include LendingClub and Prosper.

3. Revenue-Based finance:

Revenue-based finance (RBF) is an alternative financing approach where investors offer cash to a firm in return for a share of its future revenues. With RBF, repayments are connected to the business's success, allowing greater flexibility compared to typical loans. This technique caters to firms with regular income sources but minimal collateral or cash flow.

4. Angel Investors and Syndicates:

Angel investors are people who donate financing to entrepreneurs in return for stock ownership. They frequently provide not just financial resources but also knowledge and business contacts. Angel investor syndicates aggregate cash from many investors to invest in businesses together. Platforms like AngelList and Gust encourage relationships between startups and angel investors.

5. Venture Debt:

Venture debt entails borrowing capital from specialist lenders who concentrate on startups and high-growth firms. Unlike standard bank loans, venture debt may have more flexible terms and repayment arrangements customized to the requirements of startups. It is commonly used to augment equity funding and provide operating money for growth.

6. Grants and Competitions:

Research grants and competitions that give financial help to businesses. Governments, charities, and organizations regularly make grants for particular sectors, research and development initiatives, or socially important businesses. Participating in business contests not only gives the possibility to win money rewards but also provides exposure and networking possibilities.

7. Incubators and Accelerators:

Joining an incubator or accelerator program may give access to money, coaching, resources, and a supportive entrepreneurial environment. These programs frequently have a competitive application procedure and pick firms with strong growth potential. In return for equity, incubators, and accelerators give assistance to help firms accomplish milestones and seek more investment.

8. Supplier or Vendor Financing:

Explore the possibilities of obtaining attractive payment arrangements with suppliers or vendors. Extended payment periods, discounts, or vendor financing agreements may reduce cash flow limitations and enable access to necessary products or services without immediate upfront expenses.

9. Pre-sales and Crowdsourced financing:

Utilize pre-sales or crowdsourced financing strategies to earn cash before releasing your product or service. This entails giving pre-orders or early access to clients, and collecting revenue to support manufacturing or development expenditures. Crowdsourced finance systems like Tilt or Ulule may support this strategy.

When contemplating crowdsourcing or other fundraising techniques, properly investigate and understand the individual needs, hazards, and legal issues involved with each choice. Develop a convincing campaign or financing proposal that effectively explains your company concept, value proposition, and prospective rewards for investors or supporters.

Remember to utilize your network, interact with your target audience, and successfully express the unique qualities and advantages of your company. These creative fundraising techniques may give not just funds but also important marketing exposure, consumer validation, and community support.

CHAPTER 7

MARKETING AND BRANDING

A. Developing a Marketing Strategy:
Promoting Your Business Effectively

Marketing plays a critical part in the success of your company by building awareness, recruiting clients, and generating revenue. This part of your book focuses on establishing a complete marketing plan to successfully advertise your firm. Let's discuss the important stages in building a marketing strategy:

1. Define Your Target Market: Identify and understand your target market—the exact set of clients who are most likely to be interested in your goods or services. Consider elements like demographics, psychographics, behavior, and needs. This insight will guide your marketing efforts and help you modify your messaging and techniques properly.

2. Conduct Market Research: Conduct extensive market research to get insights into your industry, rivals, and client preferences. Analyze

market trends, consumer behavior, and competition environment to uncover opportunities and optimize your marketing strategy. This study will guide your marketing choices and help you distinguish your firm from the competition.

3. Set Clear Marketing Objectives: Establish precise, measurable, attainable, relevant, and time-bound (SMART) marketing objectives connected with your overall company goals. These aims may include improving brand exposure, generating leads, driving website traffic, enhancing revenue, or expanding into new areas. Clearly explain what you intend to accomplish via your marketing efforts.

4. Craft a Unique Value Proposition: Develop a clear and compelling value proposition that conveys the unique advantages and value your firm gives to clients. Highlight what sets you unique from the competition and why buyers should select your goods or services. Your value proposition should connect with your target market and solve their pain points or wants.

5. Choose Effective Marketing Channels: Select the marketing channels that are most relevant and successful in reaching your target demographic. These may include digital channels like as websites, search engine optimization (SEO), social media, email marketing, content marketing, and online advertising. Traditional mediums including print media, radio, television, and outdoor advertising may also be acceptable depending on your target demographic.

6. Develop a material Marketing Strategy: Content marketing entails developing and sharing useful and relevant material to attract and engage your target audience. Develop a content marketing plan that includes blog posts, articles, videos, infographics, and other types of material that educate, entertain, or inspire your audience. Consistently provide high-quality content that demonstrates your knowledge and establishes confidence with your consumers.

7. Utilize Social Media: Leverage social media channels to connect with your target audience, develop brand recognition, and communicate with consumers. Choose the social media networks that fit with your target

market and industry. Develop a social media plan that involves frequent posting, community involvement, offering quality information, running targeted advertisements, and monitoring comments or reviews.

8. Implement Search Engine Optimization (SEO): Optimize your website and online content to boost your exposure and ranking in search engine results. Conduct keyword research, improve your website structure, develop great content, and get backlinks from credible sources. A well-executed SEO plan may boost organic traffic to your website and enhance your online visibility.

9. Build Relationships with Influencers: Collaborate with influencers or industry experts who have a substantial following and impact in your target market. Partnering with influencers may help grow your reach, create a reputation, and generate interaction with your business. Identify influencers that agree with your brand values and develop honest partnerships that benefit both sides.

10. Monitor and Analyze Results: Continuously monitor and assess the success of your marketing activities. Use analytics tools to measure website traffic, engagement metrics, conversion rates, and sales. Adjust your marketing plan depending on the data and insights you acquire, recognizing what is performing effectively and areas that want better.

Remember, your marketing approach should be dynamic and responsive. Stay updated on evolving marketing trends, technology, and client preferences. Continuously tweak and optimize your marketing efforts to remain ahead of the competition and efficiently reach your target demographic.

B. Branding Your Business:
Creating a Distinctive and Memorable Brand

Branding is a vital component of your business's success since it helps distinguish your goods or services from rivals and affects how people view your organization. This portion of your book focuses on branding methods to develop a powerful and memorable brand identity. Let's review the important stages in branding your business:

1. Define Your Brand Identity: Start by identifying your brand's distinctive identity. Identify your brand values, purpose, and vision. Determine the personality traits and attributes that fit with your company. Consider how you want your target audience to view your brand—whether it's inventive, dependable, entertaining, or professional. This clarity will guide your branding initiatives.

2. Create a Memorable Brand Name: Choose a brand name that is unique, memorable, and linked with your company. Consider variables such as the availability of domain names, trademark concerns, and the significance of the name to your goods or services. Conduct a thorough investigation to confirm your selected name is not already in use by another company.

3. Design a Compelling Logo: Your logo is a visual representation of your business and should be developed to suit your brand identity. Hire a professional designer or agency to develop a logo that is original, aesthetically attractive, and memorable. Ensure that your logo is adaptable and may be efficiently utilized across numerous platforms and marketing materials.

4. Develop a Brand Voice and Messaging: Define the tone and style of communication for your brand. Determine how your brand should sound when communicating with customers—whether it's informal and welcoming, professional and authoritative, or somewhere in between. Create brand message standards to promote consistent and unified communication across all mediums.

5. Design Consistent Branding Elements: Establish consistent branding components across all consumer touchpoints. This includes your website, packaging, marketing materials, social media accounts, and any other venues where your brand is displayed. Maintain consistent colors, font, and visual design to promote brand awareness and provide a cohesive brand experience.

6. Craft a Brand Narrative: Develop a compelling brand narrative that connects with your target audience. Communicate your brand's history, beliefs, and purpose in a manner that engages and connects with people

on an emotional level. Your brand narrative should convey authenticity and establish a feeling of loyalty and trust among your audience.

7. Build Brand Recognition: Implement marketing methods to boost brand recognition and exposure. Leverage social media channels, content marketing, search engine optimization (SEO), and online advertising to reach your target audience. Participate at industry events, sponsor relevant activities, and connect with influencers to enhance your brand's exposure.

8. Deliver Consistent Brand Experience: Ensure that every encounter consumer have with your brand gives a consistent and enjoyable experience. From customer service contacts to product packaging and user experience, aim for excellence at every touchpoint. Consistency generates trust and supports your brand's reputation.

9. build Brand Loyalty: Build great ties with your consumers to build brand loyalty. Provide great goods or services, surpass consumer expectations, and create unique experiences. Implement loyalty programs, customer awards, or special offers to promote repeat purchases and build long-term customer connections.

10. Monitor and Evolve Your Brand: Continuously monitor the impression of your brand and obtain input from consumers. Regularly analyze the performance of your branding initiatives and make required improvements to remain current and competitive. Adapt your branding approach as your firm develops and as client preferences change.

Remember, branding is a long-term investment that demands consistency and devotion. Stay loyal to your brand identity, execute your brand promise, and actively connect with your target audience to establish a powerful and memorable brand.

C. Building an Online Presence:
Establishing Your Business in the Digital World

In today's digital world, having a strong online presence is vital for the success of your organization. This part of your book focuses on developing a successful online presence to reach and connect with your target audience.

Let's review the important stages in building your company in the digital world:

1. Develop a Professional Website: Create a user-friendly and aesthetically beautiful website that portrays your business. Ensure that your website is mobile-responsive since a rising number of visitors access the internet via mobile devices. Include crucial information about your organization, goods or services, contact data, and unambiguous calls to action.

2. Optimize for Search Engines: Implement search engine optimization (SEO) tactics to boost your website's visibility in search engine results. Research relevant keywords and include them in your website's content, meta tags, and headers. Generate high-quality backlinks from respected websites to boost your website's authority.

3. Leverage Social Media channels: Create company accounts on key social media channels where your target audience is engaged. Establish a regular brand presence, publish compelling material, and communicate with your audience. Choose the platforms that correspond with your company objectives and the tastes of your target audience.

4. Develop a material Marketing Strategy: Create quality and relevant material that educates, entertains, or solves issues for your target audience. This may include blog entries, articles, videos, infographics, podcasts, and more. Regularly post and promote your content to attract and engage your audience, presenting your brand as an expert in your sector.

5. Engage in Social Listening and Monitoring: Actively listen to online discussions about your industry, brand, or goods. Use social listening tools to track mentions, hashtags, and debates. Respond to consumer comments, answer problems, and participate in discussions to establish connections and show your dedication to customer satisfaction.

6. Implement Email Marketing: Build an email list of interested prospects and current clients. Send frequent emails, updates, promotions, and targeted offers to cultivate your connections with subscribers. Use email marketing solutions to automate campaigns and measure engagement data, such as open rates and click-through rates.

7. Explore Online Advertising: Consider online advertising solutions to improve brand exposure and attract targeted visitors to your website. Platforms like Google Ads and social media advertising platforms provide different ad styles, targeting possibilities, and budget flexibility. Set defined targets and analyze the success of your advertisements to improve your advertising strategy.

8. Engage in Influencer Marketing: Collaborate with influencers or industry experts who have a big following and impact in your target market. Partnering with influencers may broaden your reach, develop your reputation, and drive interest in your goods or services. Identify influencers whose ideals connect with your business and harness their reach and engagement.

9. Monitor Online Reputation: Regularly monitor and manage your online reputation by checking online reviews, social media mentions, and comments. Respond swiftly and professionally to consumer comments, both good and negative. Address consumer complaints and address problems to retain a great brand reputation.

10. Measure and Analyze Performance: Utilize analytics tools to monitor the performance of your online operations. Monitor website traffic, social media interaction, email campaign stats, and online conversions. Analyze the data to acquire insights into what tactics and channels are delivering success. Adjust your strategy depending on the facts to maximize your online visibility.

Remember, developing your internet presence needs ongoing work, involvement, and adaptability. Stay up to speed with digital marketing trends, consumer preferences, and new technologies to successfully interact with your target audience online.

D. Traditional Marketing Techniques:
Reaching Your Audience Beyond the Digital World

While digital marketing has acquired substantial popularity, conventional marketing strategies still maintain significance in reaching a bigger audience. This part of your book focuses on conventional marketing strategies that may complement your internet efforts and help you connect with your target audience. Let's analyze some successful classic marketing techniques:

1. Print Advertising: Consider putting advertising in newspapers, magazines, and related print media that your target demographic reads. Craft intriguing ad language and utilize eye-catching imagery to gain attention and express your message successfully. Ensure that your adverts connect with your brand identity and message.

2. Direct Mail: Utilize direct mail campaigns to contact prospective consumers directly in their mailboxes. Develop aesthetically beautiful and customized mailings that showcase your unique selling features and offer a clear call to action. Use tailored mailing lists to guarantee that your mailers reach the most appropriate audience.

3. Outdoor Advertising: Explore outdoor advertising choices like billboards, bus stop advertisements, banners, and signs in high-traffic locations. Choose sites wisely depending on your target audience's demographics and habits. Use appealing images and simple content to catch attention and increase brand recognition.

4. Event Marketing: Participate in trade fairs, conferences, community events, and exhibits relevant to your sector. Set up a booth or display to market your goods or services. Engage with attendees, offer advertising materials, and gather leads. Sponsor or organize your events to showcase your company as an industry leader and develop significant relationships.

5. Broadcast Advertising: Consider radio and television advertising to reach a large audience. Create captivating audio or video advertising that delivers your business message successfully within the allowed time. Choose broadcasting networks and periods that fit with your target audience's preferences.

6. Public Relations (PR): Build connections with media outlets and journalists to get publicity and news releases about your firm. Develop noteworthy tales, milestones, or events that are important and engaging

to the public. Utilize press releases, media kits, and media pitching to achieve good media attention.

7. Networking and Referrals: Attend industry conferences, networking events, and business meetings to interact with people in your sector. Build ties with possible partners, suppliers, and consumers. Encourage pleased clients to promote your company to their networks via referral programs or incentives.

8. Branded stuff: Create branded stuff such as pens, t-shirts, mugs, or keychains to distribute at events, trade exhibitions, or as handouts. This helps improve brand awareness and acts as a reminder of your company in the everyday lives of your target audience.

9. Print Collateral: Design and distribute printed pieces like brochures, flyers, and business cards that give succinct and persuasive information about your goods or services. Ensure that your print material matches your brand identity and corresponds with your entire marketing plan.

10. Public Speaking and Sponsorship: Seek chances to speak at industry events, conferences, or educational institutions. Establish yourself as an authority in your subject by sharing your expertise and ideas. Consider supporting local events, sports teams, or philanthropic initiatives that appeal to your target demographic and increase your brand image.

Remember, conventional marketing approaches should be incorporated strategically with your total marketing strategy. Analyze your target demographic, objectives, and budget to decide which conventional marketing approaches are most successful for reaching and engaging your unique audience.

E. Social Media Marketing:
Leveraging the Power of Social Platforms

Social media has altered the way companies communicate with their audience, generate brand recognition, and engage consumers. This portion of your book focuses on social media marketing tactics to properly leverage popular social networks for your company. Let's investigate how you can use the power of social media:

1. Choose the Right Sites: Identify the social media sites that correspond with your target demographic and company goals. Consider networks like Facebook, Instagram, Twitter, LinkedIn, Pinterest, and YouTube. Each platform caters to various demographics and content types, so select carefully depending on your audience's preferences.
2. Create a Consistent Brand Presence: Establish a coherent brand presence across all social media channels. Use consistent branding components such as your logo, color scheme, and tone of voice. Maintain a professional and interesting profile that represents your brand identity.
3. Develop a Content plan: Create a content plan that connects with your brand and resonates with your target audience. Plan and produce content that informs entertains, or inspires your audience. Use a combination of forms including photographs, videos, infographics, and blog entries to keep your material entertaining and different.
4. Engage with Your Audience: Actively engage with your followers by replying to comments, messages, and mentions. Encourage dialogues, ask questions, and seek feedback. Show genuine interest in your audience's thoughts and establish a feeling of community around your business.
5. Leverage Influencer Marketing: Collaborate with social media influencers that have a big following and impact on your target market. Partner with influencers that connect with your brand values and have an engaged audience. Sponsored articles, product reviews, and influencer takeovers may help extend your reach and reputation.
6. Execute targeted Ad Campaigns: Utilize social media advertising channels to execute targeted ad campaigns. Define your target audience based on demographics, interests, and habits. Set defined goals for your initiatives, whether it's brand exposure, lead generation, or driving conversions. Monitor and tweak your campaigns for optimal performance.
7. Utilize Hashtags: Incorporate relevant hashtags into your social media postings to boost their exposure and reach. Research popular hashtags

in your business and apply them carefully to get a bigger audience. Create customized hashtags to promote user-generated content and improve brand interaction.

8. Analyze Performance and Adjust: Use social media analytics tools to monitor the performance of your social media activities. Monitor crucial metrics like engagement, reach, clicks, and conversions. Analyze the data to discover effective tactics and areas for improvement. Make data-driven judgments and adapt your social media approach appropriately.

9. Stay Consistently Active: Consistency is crucial in social media marketing. Regularly upload compelling material, connect with your audience, and remain up to speed with the newest trends and topics in your field. Develop a content calendar to maintain a constant publication schedule.

10. Monitor and Manage Online Reputation: Regularly monitor social media mentions and discussions about your brand. Respond swiftly to both good and negative comments, resolving problems and displaying your dedication to client satisfaction. Engage in reputation management by keeping a favorable brand image online.

Remember, social media is a dynamic and ever-evolving medium. Stay updated on the newest features, algorithm updates, and trends on each social networking site. Continuously change your social media approach to fit the changing demands and preferences of your audience.

F. Public Relations and Advertising:
Enhancing Your Brand Visibility

Public relations (PR) and advertising play vital roles in boosting your brand exposure, maintaining your reputation, and reaching a larger audience. This portion of your book focuses on using PR and advertising methods efficiently. Let's investigate how you can leverage these tactics to advertise your business:

1. Public Relations (PR) Strategy:

- Define Your PR Objectives: Determine the objectives you want to accomplish via PR activities, such as growing brand recognition, producing good media coverage, or portraying oneself as an industry expert.
- Develop Key statements: Craft key statements that match your brand identity and resonate with your target audience. These messages should represent your unique selling characteristics and the value your firm delivers.
- Build Media Relationships: Establish ties with journalists, bloggers, and influencers in your field. Provide them with relevant information, story ideas, and press releases that correspond with their interests and target audience.
- Press Releases and Media Kits: Create appealing press releases and media kits to provide noteworthy details about your business, product launches, corporate milestones, or industry insights. Distribute them to appropriate media outlets and journalists to create media attention.
- Media Interviews and Guest Blogging: Seek chances to be interviewed by the media or offer guest blog pieces to respectable websites. Share your skills, thoughts, and unique viewpoints to obtain visibility and create respect in your business.
2. Advertising Strategy:
- Define Your Target Audience: Clearly define your target audience and their demographics, interests, and activities. This will help you identify the most successful advertising channels and design captivating ad messaging.
- Select Advertising Channels: Consider numerous advertising channels such as print media, radio, television, outdoor billboards, internet advertising platforms, and social media commercials. Choose the channels that best fit your target demographic and budget.
- Design Engaging advertising: Create aesthetically attractive and engaging advertising that successfully expresses your business message. Tailor your ad text and imagery to connect with your target audience's wants, desires, and pain points.

- Set Advertising Budget and Objectives: Determine your advertising budget depending on your company's resources and objectives. Set precise objectives such as improving brand exposure, generating website traffic, or enhancing sales conversions.
- Monitor and Optimize: Continuously monitor the success of your advertising initiatives. Track critical data like as impressions, click-through rates, conversion rates, and return on investment (ROI). Make data-driven choices to improve your ad campaigns for better outcomes.
3. Integrated Marketing Communications:
- Create a Consistent Brand Voice: Ensure that your PR efforts, advertising campaigns, and other marketing activities retain a consistent brand voice and message. This helps establish your brand identity and develop trust with your audience.
- Cross-Promotion: Explore chances to cross-promote your PR activities and advertising campaigns. For example, you may display media coverage on your website or social media channels, or integrate your key messaging into your commercials.
- Leverage Social Media: Use social media channels to magnify your PR efforts and market your brand. Share media coverage, news releases, and promotional information on your social media networks to reach a broader audience.
5. Sponsorships and Partnerships:
- Identify Relevant Opportunities: Consider sponsoring events, community activities, or industry conferences that connect with your brand values and target demographic. Seek relationships with related firms or influencers to enhance your exposure and tap into their current audience.
- Collaborate with Charities or Non-Profit groups: Align your brand with philanthropic causes or non-profit groups that resonate with your target demographic. This may increase your brand's reputation and promote a good public attitude.

Remember to frequently review the efficacy of your PR and advertising activities. Monitor media coverage, ad performance, and audience input to make required modifications and enhancements. By establishing a well-rounded PR and advertising plan, you can successfully boost your brand exposure and engage with your target audience.

CHAPTER 8

SALES AND CUSTOMER ACQUISITION

A. Sales Techniques and Approaches:

Mastering the Art of Selling

In the competitive corporate world, understanding efficient sales strategies is vital for recruiting clients and growing revenue. This part of your book focuses on numerous sales strategies and approaches that may help your complete transactions and develop enduring client connections. Let's discuss some essential techniques:

1. Consultative Selling: Adopt a consultative approach to sales by concentrating on knowing your client's requirements, issues, and ambitions. Ask probing inquiries to understand their problem spots and

personalize your answers appropriately. Position yourself as a trustworthy expert who delivers excellent insights and suggestions.

2. Relationship creating: Prioritize creating solid ties with your consumers. Invest time in getting to know them personally and understanding their companies. Demonstrate real interest and empathy, and establish long-term friendships based on trust and mutual respect.

3. Active Listening: Practice active listening skills to genuinely comprehend your clients' worries and ambitions. Give them your complete attention, ask clarifying questions, and paraphrase their comments to ensure you know their requirements properly. This helps create rapport and allows you to give customized solutions.

4. Effective Communication: Develop great communication abilities to explain your value proposition clearly and convincingly. Adapt your communication approach to accommodate each customer's preferences and personality. Use clear and appealing language that connects with your audience.

5. Feature-Benefit Selling: Highlight the distinctive qualities of your product or service and convert them into actual advantages for the consumer. Show how your service tackles their unique pain areas and delivers value to their company. Emphasize the consequences and benefits they may anticipate.

6. Overcoming Objections: Anticipate and handle client objections proactively. Listen intently to their worries and reply with well-prepared responses that assuage their uncertainties. Present case studies, testimonials, or statistics to back your assertions and offer confidence.

7. Building a Sales Pipeline: Implement a systematic strategy to lead creation and sales pipeline management. Identify and qualify prospective prospects, nurture them through the sales funnel, and follow up regularly. Utilize customer relationship management (CRM) solutions to log interactions and remain organized.

8. Effective Negotiation: Master the art of negotiating by identifying mutually beneficial solutions. Prepare well, understand your intended

results, and be prepared to compromise when required. Focus on generating a win-win situation that satisfies both sides.

9. Upselling and Cross-Selling: Identify chances to upsell or cross-sell new items or services to current clients. Understand their increasing demands and make personalized suggestions that improve their experience and address new challenges.

10. constant Learning and Improvement: Sales strategies develop with time, so commit to constant learning and improvement. Stay current on market developments, sales tactics, and new technology that may boost your sales performance. Seek input from clients and coworkers to enhance your strategy.

Remember, great sales approaches involve a mix of talent, knowledge, and practice. Adapt and modify your strategy depending on client feedback and market circumstances. By concentrating on creating connections, understanding client requirements, and offering value, you may become a trusted sales professional and achieve consistent sales success.

B. Building Customer Relationships:
Fostering Loyalty and Repeat Business

Building solid customer connections is crucial for long-term company success. This part of your book focuses on tactics and ways to develop lasting relationships with your clients and drive repeat business. Let's review some essential methods for creating customer relationships:

1. Customer-Centric Approach: Adopt a customer-centric approach, where your major emphasis is on fulfilling and exceeding customer demands and expectations. Make client happiness and joy a primary priority in every engagement and transaction.

2. Personalization: Treat each consumer as an individual by tailoring your interactions. Use consumer data and insights to adapt your services and communication to their preferences and requirements. Address them by name and show genuine interest in their individual wants.

3. Timely and Responsive Communication: Respond to consumer inquiries, comments, and concerns immediately and courteously. Use several contact methods, such as email, phone, and live chat, to provide accessibility and ease. Be proactive in reaching out to customers to give updates or fix any difficulties.

4. Consistency in Service: Strive for consistency in offering high-quality service across all client touchpoints. Train your personnel to create a smooth and great experience throughout the client journey. Set and maintain service standards that represent your brand values.

5. Relationship-Building Activities: Go beyond transactional contacts by participating in relationship-building activities. Send customized thank-you cards, birthday greetings, or holiday wishes to demonstrate gratitude and establish a feeling of connection. Consider creating client appreciation events or unique promos to improve ties.

6. Customer input and Surveys: Seek input from your consumers on their experience with your goods or services. Conduct surveys or utilize online review services to obtain their comments and ideas. Actively listen to their comments, make modifications based on their advice, and convey the steps you do.

7. Loyalty Programs: Implement loyalty programs that reward clients for their recurring business. Offer incentives, discounts, or exclusive access to special offerings or events. Encourage clients to suggest your company to others and give rewards for successful referrals.

8. Continuous Value Creation: Strive to consistently deliver value to your consumers beyond the original transaction. Offer continuous assistance, instructional tools, or special content that helps them realize the advantages of your goods or services. Demonstrate your knowledge and devotion to their achievement.

9. Proactive Relationship Management: Actively maintain customer connections by frequently reaching out to check in on their happiness and discover any developing requirements. Offer proactive suggestions or improvements based on their use habits or evolving needs.

10. Resolve concerns with Empathy: Inevitably, concerns or complaints may occur. Handle these circumstances with empathy, thoughtfulness, and dedication to reaching a good settlement. Show genuine care for the customer's experience and strive towards a mutually beneficial result.

Remember, creating good customer connections requires time, effort, and persistent attention. Focus on establishing a great client experience that extends beyond the purchase. By fostering trust, individualized communication, and continual value creation, you can promote client loyalty, drive repeat business, and produce good word-of-mouth.

C. Effective Communication and Negotiation:
Building Trust and Closing Deals

Effective communication and negotiating abilities are necessary for sales professionals to create rapport, understand client demands, and effectively conclude transactions. This portion of your book focuses on approaches and strategies to boost your communication and negotiating talents. Let's discuss some crucial practices:

1. Active Listening: Listen intently to your clients to completely grasp their requirements, issues, and goals. Avoid interrupting and offer verbal or non-verbal indicators to convey that you are attentive and interested. Paraphrase or summarize their words to ensure you have a clear grasp of their stance.
2. Clear and short Communication: Clearly explain your point utilizing simple and short language. Avoid jargon or technical terminology that may confuse the buyer. Use visual aids, stories, or examples to demonstrate your views and make complicated concepts more clear.
3. Empathy and Emotional Intelligence: Develop empathy for your consumers by putting yourself in their position. Understand their emotions, motives, and obstacles. Show empathy in your communication by recognizing their sentiments and giving assistance or ideas that solve their problems.

4. Building Rapport: Establishing a true connection with your consumers helps establish trust and deepens the sales relationship. Find common ground, show interest in their personal or professional life, and use open-ended inquiries to stimulate discourse. Mirror their body language and conversational style to develop rapport.

5. Non-Verbal Communication: Pay attention to your non-verbal indicators, such as facial expressions, body posture, and gestures. Maintain eye contact, assume an open and inviting stance, and utilize suitable hand gestures to emphasize your message. Be conscious of the customer's non-verbal clues to measure their degree of attention and participation.

6. Persuasive Communication: Develop persuasive communication abilities to successfully influence consumer choices. Highlight the advantages and value of your product or service, stressing how it addresses their unique difficulties or satisfies their needs. Use narrative and case studies to highlight good results.

7. Building Trust and Credibility: Earn the trust and develop credibility by being honest, truthful, and dependable in your communication. Provide correct information, satisfy your obligations, and follow through on pledges. Share testimonials, client success stories, or industry honors to illustrate your track record.

8. Effective Questioning: Ask strategic questions to find client demands, pain areas, and purchase motives. Use a blend of open-ended and closed-ended questions to acquire information and direct the discussion. Ask probing inquiries that urge the consumer to think deeper and express their difficulties.

9. Negotiation Strategies: Master negotiating strategies to achieve mutually beneficial deals with your consumers. Prepare in advance by knowing your customer's goals, restrictions, and options. Focus on generating win-win solutions that meet all sides' interests. Aim for cooperation rather than conflict.

10. Handling concerns: Anticipate and resolve consumer concerns efficiently. Rather than ignoring criticisms, utilize them as a chance to

give further information or explanation. Understand the underlying problems and modify your solutions appropriately. Offer proof, testimonials, or promises to assuage concerns.

Remember, successful communication and negotiating skills are acquired via practice, feedback, and ongoing growth. Adapt your strategy depending on the customer's communication style and preferences. By mastering these abilities, you can develop trust, influence choices, and conclude agreements effectively.

D. Customer Acquisition Strategies:
Reaching and Converting Prospects

Customer acquisition is a vital component of expanding your company. This portion of your book focuses on successful tactics to reach and convert prospective consumers into paying clients. Let's analyze some significant consumer acquisition strategies:

1. Targeted Marketing Campaigns: Identify your target market and design focused marketing strategies to attract prospective clients. Utilize multiple marketing platforms such as social media, search engine optimization (SEO), content marketing, email marketing, and paid advertising to raise awareness and generate leads.
2. material Marketing: Create interesting and informative material that connects with your target audience. Publish blog entries, articles, videos, or podcasts that address their issue areas, give answers, and demonstrate your expertise. Distribute this material via your website, social media platforms, and other relevant avenues.
3. Search Engine Optimization (SEO): Optimize your website and content to boost your presence in search engine results. Conduct keyword research to determine the words and phrases your target audience is looking for. Incorporate these keywords into your website content, meta tags, and headlines to improve organic traffic.
4. Social Media Marketing: Leverage social media channels to interact with your target audience and promote your brand. Create a strong

presence on platforms that coincide with your target market. Share compelling material, engage in relevant debates, and create connections with prospective consumers via social media interactions.

5. Paid Advertising: Consider utilizing paid advertising channels such as Google advertisements, social network advertisements, or display advertising to reach a bigger audience. Set unique targeting settings based on demographics, hobbies, and online activity to guarantee your advertising is viewed by suitable prospects.

6. Referral Programs: Encourage your pleased clients to suggest your company to their friends, family, and professional networks. Offer incentives, such as discounts, awards, or special advantages, to both the referrer and the recommended consumer. Word-of-mouth referrals may be incredibly helpful in obtaining new clients.

7. collaborations and Collaborations: Explore collaborations with related firms or influencers in your sector. Co-create content, conduct joint events or cross-promote each other's services to tap into new client bases. Collaborations may assist in boosting your brand exposure and reputation.

8. Lead Generation Campaigns: Develop lead-generating initiatives to gather the contact information of prospective consumers. Offer useful stuff, like eBooks, whitepapers, or webinars, in return for their email address or other pertinent data. Nurture these prospects with targeted email marketing efforts.

9. Networking and Industry Events: Attend industry conferences, trade exhibitions, and networking events to engage with prospective consumers face-to-face. Engage in meaningful talks, exchange business cards, and follow up later to prolong the connection. Networking may lead to lucrative recommendations and collaborations.

10. examine and Optimize: Continuously examine the performance of your client acquisition efforts. Monitor critical indicators, such as website traffic, conversion rates, cost per lead, and client acquisition cost. Use data-driven insights to improve your marketing and allocate money to the most effective channels.

Remember, client acquisition is a constant process that demands consistent effort and adaptability. Monitor industry developments, client preferences, and competition activity to remain ahead. By implementing a mix of targeted marketing, content production, strategic alliances, and data-driven optimization, you can successfully gain new consumers and build your company.

E. Retaining and Upselling to Existing Customers:
Maximizing Customer Lifetime Value

Retaining and upselling to current clients is a cost-effective method to improve revenue and optimize the lifetime value of each customer. This portion of your book focuses on techniques to create client loyalty, cultivate relationships, and stimulate future purchases. Let's discuss some essential methods for keeping and upselling to current customers:

1. Exceptional Customer Service: Provide great customer service at every touchpoint. Be responsive, sensitive, and compassionate to customer requirements and concerns. Aim to surpass customer expectations and create unforgettable experiences that separate your firm from the competition.
2. Personalized Communication: Tailor your message to each customer's tastes and demands. Use consumer data to segment your client base and give targeted communications, offers, and suggestions. Leverage automation techniques to expand personalization while preserving a human touch.
3. Customer Loyalty Programs: Implement customer loyalty programs to reward and promote repeat business. Offer special discounts, incentives, or awards to consumers depending on their purchasing history or involvement. Encourage clients to remain loyal to your brand and recommend others to your company.
4. frequent involvement: Stay connected with your clients via frequent involvement. Use email marketing, social media, or SMS campaigns to distribute useful material, product updates, or special offers. Keep your

brand top-of-mind and develop connections even when people are not actively shopping.

5. Proactive Customer Support: Anticipate and handle consumer concerns before they become problems. Monitor consumer feedback, perform satisfaction surveys, and utilize analytics to uncover possible trouble areas. Be proactive in reaching out to consumers to give support, rectify problems, or provide more value.

6. Cross-Selling and Upselling: Identify possibilities to cross-sell or upsell to current clients. Recommend supplementary items or services that improve their initial purchase. Offer upgrade choices or bundle packages that give extra value. Communicate the advantages of these extra solutions clearly and link them with consumer demands.

7. unique discounts and Upgrades: Reward your loyal consumers with unique discounts, early access to new items or features, or special upgrades. Make them feel valued and appreciated for their continuous assistance. This may create a feeling of exclusivity and stimulate repeat purchasing.

8. Relationship creating: Invest in creating strong ties with your current consumers. Engage in meaningful discussions, take a real interest in their company or personal success, and express thanks for their continuous support. Building a solid rapport may lead to long-term loyalty and recommendations.

9. Customer input and Surveys: Continuously seek input from your current consumers to understand their shifting requirements and expectations. Conduct frequent satisfaction surveys or utilize consumer feedback portals to obtain information. Use this input to create adjustments and indicate that you appreciate their thoughts.

10. Ongoing Value Creation: Continuously deliver value to your current consumers beyond the first transaction. Offer extra tools, instructional information, or special incentives that help customers reach their objectives or solve their difficulties. Position your firm as a trustworthy adviser and partner in their success.

Remember, keeping and upselling to current clients involves continual work and attention. Treat each consumer as a long-term partnership and engage in developing that connection. By offering outstanding customer service, customizing communication, introducing loyalty programs, and proactively interacting with customers, you may enhance customer loyalty, promote repeat business, and uncover extra income potential.

CHAPTER 9

OPERATIONS AND LOGISTICS

A. Managing Day-to-Day Operations:
Ensuring Efficiency and Effectiveness

Managing day-to-day operations is vital for the seamless operation of your organization. This part of your book focuses on critical factors and best practices for efficiently managing your business. Let's investigate some essential aspects:

1. Operational Planning: Develop a comprehensive operational plan that describes the duties, responsibilities, and procedures necessary to manage your organization. Define important goals, specify performance criteria, and establish timetables. Regularly examine and update your operating strategy to react to changing conditions.
2. Workflow and Process Optimization: Streamline your workflows and processes to boost efficiency and productivity. Identify bottlenecks, minimize superfluous procedures, and automate repeated activities

whenever feasible. Implement technological solutions and technologies that assist efficient operations.

3. Resource Allocation: Allocate resources efficiently to fulfill operational needs. Ensure you have the proper staff, equipment, and supplies to carry out your company tasks. Monitor resource use and make modifications as required to enhance efficiency.

4. Inventory Management: Implement an inventory management system to monitor and regulate your inventory levels. Regularly monitor demand trends, estimate future requirements, and define reorder points to ensure you have an appropriate supply without surplus inventory. Use technology to automate inventory tracking and replenishment operations.

5. Quality Control and Assurance: Establish quality control procedures to verify that your goods or services meet or exceed client expectations. Implement quality standards, perform frequent inspections, and monitor customer feedback. Continuously upgrade your processes to better product or service quality.

6. Customer Relationship Management (CRM): Implement a CRM system to organize and track customer interactions, queries, and comments. Use CRM data to acquire insights into consumer preferences, purchase history, and communication history. Leverage this knowledge to better customer service and develop stronger connections.

7. Vendor and Supplier Management: Develop good ties with your vendors and suppliers. Negotiate advantageous conditions, keep open channels of contact, and frequently review their performance. Ensure a dependable supply chain and identify potential for cost reductions and process improvements.

8. Risk Management: Identify and minimize any hazards that might damage your operations. Conduct risk assessments, build contingency plans, and apply relevant protections. Regularly examine and adapt your risk management methods to handle evolving challenges.

9. Performance Monitoring and Analysis: Establish key performance indicators (KPIs) to assess the performance of your activities. Monitor

and evaluate relevant data to discover opportunities for improvement. Use performance metrics to measure progress, discover patterns, and make data-driven choices.

10. Continued Improvement: Foster a culture of continual improvement inside your firm. Encourage comments and recommendations from workers at all levels. Regularly assess procedures, request suggestions for efficiency improvements, and implement changes that contribute to continual operational improvement.

By properly managing your day-to-day operations, you can boost productivity, cut expenses, and give constant value to your customers. Prioritize operational planning, improve processes, guarantee resource allocation, and apply quality control procedures. Embrace digital solutions and data-driven decision-making to achieve operational excellence.

B. Inventory Management:
Ensuring Optimal Stock Levels and Efficiency

Effective inventory management is critical for maintaining acceptable stock levels while reducing costs and optimizing operational efficiency. This portion of your book examines fundamental ideas and tactics for managing your inventory successfully. Let's look into the main parts of inventory management:

1. Inventory Classification: Classify your inventory based on characteristics such as demand, value, and turnover. Common inventory categories include raw materials, work-in-progress (WIP), completed items, and spare components. Categorizing inventory helps prioritize management efforts and distribute resources appropriately.
2. Demand Forecasting: Utilize historical data, industry trends, and consumer insights to anticipate demand for your goods or services. Accurate demand forecasting helps you identify ideal stock levels, schedule production, and minimize stockouts or overstock situations. Consider employing statistical models, market research, and consumer feedback to increase prediction accuracy.

3. Reorder Point and Safety Stock: Set a reorder point that initiates replenishment when inventory reaches a predefined level. Consider lead times, demand variations, and supplier dependability when establishing the reorder threshold. Additionally, keep a safety stock to cater for unanticipated swings in demand or supply chain interruptions.

4. Just-in-Time (JIT) Inventory: Implement JIT inventory management concepts to eliminate excess inventory and related expenses. JIT strives to synchronize production with demand, avoiding the need for huge inventory buffers. This method demands tight coordination with suppliers, efficient manufacturing processes, and dependable logistics.

5. Inventory monitoring Systems: Employ inventory monitoring systems to monitor stock levels, track movement, and spot inconsistencies. Utilize barcode scanners, radio frequency identification (RFID), or inventory management software to automate data collecting and simplify inventory tracking operations.

6. ABC Analysis: Perform an ABC analysis to prioritize inventory management activities depending on the value and use frequency of products. Classify things as A (high-value, high-usage), B (moderate-value, moderate-usage), or C (low-value, low-usage). Allocate extra attention to managing high-value products to avoid stockouts and decrease carrying costs.

7. Inventory Turnover and Carrying Costs: Calculate inventory turnover ratios to analyze how rapidly your inventory is sold and restocked. High inventory turnover suggests effective stock management. Conversely, monitor carrying costs, including storage, insurance, and obsolescence fees, to reduce spending associated with excess inventory.

8. Supplier Collaboration: Collaborate closely with your suppliers to maximize inventory management. Establish effective communication channels, discuss demand projections, and negotiate advantageous conditions, such as minimum order quantities and lead times. Foster solid partnerships to guarantee timely delivery and control supply chain risks.

9. frequent Audits and Cycle Counts: Conduct frequent inventory audits and cycle counts to ensure stock correctness and discover inconsistencies. Implement effective inventory control methods, such as physical counts, reconciliation with system records, and examination of deviations. Regular audits assist in preserving data integrity and avoid inventory inconsistencies.
10. Continuous Improvement: Continuously analyze and improve your inventory management procedures. Analyze data, identify opportunities for improvement, and execute process upgrades. Leverage technology and automation technologies, like as inventory management software and demand planning systems, to simplify inventory management procedures.

By using good inventory management procedures, you may optimize stock levels, decrease carrying costs, avoid stockouts, and increase overall operational efficiency. Prioritize demand forecasts, establish reorder points, use monitoring tools, and coordinate with suppliers to maintain efficient and well-controlled inventory management.

C. Supply Chain and Logistics:
Efficiently Managing the Flow of Goods and Services

An effective and well-managed supply chain and logistics system is vital for maintaining the seamless movement of products and services from suppliers to consumers. This part of your book discusses essential concerns and best practices for improving your supply chain and logistics operations. Let's look into the main parts of supply chain and logistics management:

1. Supply Chain Design: Design an efficient supply chain network that matches with your company objectives and consumer requests. Consider aspects such as sourcing, manufacturing, storage, transportation, and distribution. Analyze multiple supply chain models, analyze trade-offs, and determine the most suited configuration for your organization.

2. Supplier Management: Establish good ties with your suppliers to guarantee timely and trustworthy delivery. Identify and qualify possible suppliers, establish contracts, and set clear expectations. Regularly monitor supplier performance and work on process enhancements to optimize the efficiency of the upstream supply chain.

3. Demand Planning and Forecasting: Use precise demand planning and forecasting tools to anticipate consumer demands and organize your supply chain appropriately. Gather and evaluate data on previous sales, market trends, and consumer preferences. Collaborate with sales and marketing departments to integrate their insights into demand forecasting.

4. Inventory Optimization: Optimize inventory levels throughout the supply chain to balance consumer demand and operational expenses. Implement inventory management strategies outlined previously, such as demand forecasting, reorder point setting, safety stock management, and just-in-time (JIT) concepts. Continuously monitor and modify inventory levels to match changing demand trends.

5. Transportation and Logistics: Develop efficient transportation and logistics methods to guarantee timely and cost-effective delivery of products. Evaluate multiple modes of transportation, such as road, rail, air, or sea, depending on parameters including distance, speed, cost, and product characteristics. Optimize routes, consolidate shipments, and utilize digital solutions to simplify logistics operations.

6. Warehouse Management: Efficiently manage your warehouses or distribution facilities to support seamless inventory movement and order fulfillment. Optimize warehouse architecture, install optimal storage methods, and apply inventory tracking technology. Use warehouse management systems (WMS) to increase inventory visibility, order accuracy, and labor efficiency.

7. Information Systems and Technology: Leverage technological solutions to boost supply chain visibility, data quality, and communication. Implement enterprise resource planning (ERP) systems, supply chain management (SCM) software, and collaboration platforms. Utilize real-

time data and analytics to make educated choices, monitor performance, and find areas for development.

8. Risk Management and Resilience: Identify and manage risks that may affect your supply chain, such as natural catastrophes, supplier disruptions, or geopolitical events. Develop contingency preparations, diversify suppliers, and build alternate transportation routes. Foster resilience through creating strong connections with key stakeholders and periodically reviewing and resolving any weaknesses.

9. Sustainability and Ethical Practices: Incorporate sustainability and ethical concerns into your supply chain activities. Ensure responsible sourcing, limit waste, and decrease carbon impact. Embrace ecologically sustainable techniques, promote fair working conditions, and emphasize ethical supplier partnerships.

10. cooperation and Continuous Improvement: Foster cooperation and information exchange among supply chain partners to maximize overall performance. Regularly engage with suppliers, customers, and logistics providers to match objectives and handle obstacles. Embrace a culture of continuous improvement, foster innovation, and seek input from stakeholders to generate continued advancements.

By properly managing your supply chain and logistics operations, you may boost customer satisfaction, cut expenses, and gain a competitive edge. Focus on establishing an effective supply chain network, managing inventory levels, simplifying transportation and logistics, and using technology for greater visibility and decision-making.

D. Quality Control and Customer Service:
Ensuring Product and Service Excellence

Maintaining high-quality goods and offering outstanding customer service is vital for the profitability and reputation of your organization. This portion of your book focuses on the significance of quality control and customer service in operations and logistics. Let's discuss the important concerns and solutions for guaranteeing product and service excellence:

1. Quality Control Systems: Implement a rigorous quality control system to monitor and maintain the quality of your goods or services. Establish quality standards, perform frequent inspections, and establish quality assurance methods. Use quality control methods and techniques such as statistical process control, Six Sigma, or Total Quality Management (TQM) concepts to detect and solve quality concerns.

2. Quality Assurance methods: Develop methods to assure consistent quality across your activities. This involves creating quality checkpoints at different phases of manufacturing or service delivery, performing frequent audits, and documenting quality methods. Train your personnel on quality standards and enable them to take responsibility for quality control.

3. Continuous Improvement: Foster a culture of continual improvement in quality control. Encourage input from consumers and staff to find areas for development. Use client complaints or comments as opportunities for learning and process improvement. Regularly examine and improve quality control processes based on data and insights.

4. Customer Satisfaction Measurement: Establish systems to monitor consumer satisfaction and receive feedback. Use surveys, focus groups, or internet reviews to evaluate consumer opinion. Analyze client comments to discover areas for improvement and resolve any complaints swiftly. Develop methods to surpass consumer expectations and develop long-term partnerships.

5. Service Level Agreements (SLAs): If your organization includes service delivery, construct Service Level Agreements (SLAs) to explicitly define the scope, quality standards, and performance indicators of your services. Set reasonable expectations with your consumers and guarantee that you regularly achieve or surpass the agreed-upon service standards.

6. Effective contact: Maintain open lines of contact with your consumers to understand their requirements and expectations. Convey product or service characteristics, delivery schedules, and any possible concerns.

Respond immediately to client inquiries or concerns and offer frequent updates on order status or service progress.

7. Customer Relationship Management (CRM): Utilize CRM systems to manage customer contacts and monitor consumer preferences, queries, and comments. Maintain a consolidated client database to enable tailored and efficient customer service. Leverage CRM data to detect customer patterns, preferences, and possibilities for upselling or cross-selling.

8. Employee Training and Empowerment: Invest in training programs to educate your personnel with the required skills to perform great customer service. Train them on product knowledge, effective communication, problem-solving, and conflict resolution. Empower your workers to make customer-focused choices and handle problems proactively.

9. Complaint Resolution and Service Recovery: Develop a defined strategy for managing consumer complaints or service problems. Train your personnel to address concerns with empathy, actively listen to consumers, and provide viable solutions. Focus on service recovery to transform a poor experience into a good one and regain client confidence.

10. Continuous Customer Feedback: Encourage consumers to submit feedback on their experiences and utilize that input to drive changes. Implement customer satisfaction surveys, online reviews, or feedback systems to obtain information. Actively react to customer input, resolve problems, and disclose measures made to improve their experience.

By emphasizing quality control and offering outstanding customer service, you can establish a loyal client base and distinguish your firm from the competition. Focus on creating effective quality control systems, continual improvement, and proactive customer interaction. Embrace a customer-centric strategy and empower your workers to surpass consumer expectations at every touchpoint.

E. Technology and Automation:
Leveraging Tools for Operational Efficiency

In today's digital age, technology and automation play a significant role in simplifying processes and enhancing efficiency. This portion of your book focuses on the integration of technology and automation in operations and logistics. Let's investigate how you may harness tools and technology to enhance your company processes:

1. Inventory Management Software: Implement inventory management software to automate and expedite inventory-related processes. Such software may help you monitor inventory levels, manage stock replenishment, produce purchase orders, and improve inventory turnover. Leverage features like barcode scanning, real-time data updates, and automatic inventory alerts for greater accuracy and efficiency.

2. Supply Chain Management Systems: Utilize supply chain management (SCM) systems to integrate and optimize diverse supply chain processes. These technologies offer end-to-end visibility, support demand planning and forecasting, manage supplier relationships, and simplify logistical operations. SCM solutions let you make educated choices, improve inventory levels, and boost communication with supply chain partners.

3. Enterprise Resource Planning (ERP) Systems: Implement an ERP system to integrate and manage important company processes, such as finance, sales, inventories, and procurement. ERP systems offer a consolidated platform for data management, process automation, and real-time reporting. They allow improved cooperation across various departments, minimize manual data input, and boost overall operational efficiency.

4. Warehouse Management Systems (WMS): Utilize warehouse management systems to enhance warehouse operations and improve inventory management. WMS systems include capabilities including inventory tracking, order picking optimization, labor management, and

warehouse layout optimization. They assist in decreasing mistakes, cutting picking time, and boosting overall warehouse efficiency.

5. Transportation Management Systems (TMS): Deploy transportation management systems to improve transportation planning and execution. TMS systems provide route optimization, load consolidation, carrier selection, and real-time shipment tracking. By automating transportation procedures, you may save costs, increase delivery schedules, and boost customer satisfaction.

6. Data Analytics and Business Intelligence: Leverage data analytics and business intelligence solutions to acquire meaningful insights from your operational data. Analyze key performance indicators (KPIs), discover trends, and make data-driven choices. Data analytics may assist in managing inventory levels, increase demand forecasting accuracy, and discover opportunities for operational improvement.

7. Internet of Things (IoT) and Sensors: Explore the potential of IoT and sensor technologies to gather real-time data and allow proactive decision-making. IoT devices and sensors can monitor machine operation, track inventory movement, and offer data for predictive maintenance. By embracing IoT, you can minimize downtime, optimize asset utilization, and improve operational efficiency.

8. Robotic Process Automation (RPA): Consider utilizing RPA to automate repetitive manual activities and enhance process efficiency. RPA software can perform data input, order processing, invoice generating, and other regular duties. By freeing up human resources from monotonous duties, you may divert their attention to higher-value initiatives.

9. Cloud Computing and Software as a Service (SaaS): Embrace cloud computing and SaaS solutions to access sophisticated software applications without the requirement for expensive IT infrastructure. Cloud-based technologies provide scalability, flexibility, and cost-effectiveness. They provide remote access, smooth collaboration, and automated software upgrades, guaranteeing you have access to the newest features and functions.

10. Cybersecurity and Data Protection: As you incorporate technology into your processes, emphasize cybersecurity and data protection. Implement rigorous security measures, such as firewalls, encryption, and frequent data backups, to preserve important corporate information. Stay informed with cybersecurity best practices and educate your personnel on data security standards.

By utilizing the power of technology and automation, you may simplify processes, cut costs, and enhance overall efficiency. Evaluate your company requirements, identify the areas where technology may have a major effect, and progressively incorporate applicable tools and processes. Continuously monitor and change your IT stack to remain ahead in the ever-evolving digital world.

CHAPTER 10

FINANCIAL MANAGEMENT

A. Budgeting and Financial Forecasting:
Setting Financial Goals and Planning for Success

Effective financial management is vital for the long-term success of your firm. This portion of your book focuses on budgeting and financial forecasting, which are crucial skills for defining financial goals, controlling costs, and preserving financial stability. Let's look into the fundamental parts of budgeting and financial forecasting:

1. Importance of Budgeting: Explain the relevance of budgeting in business. Budgeting helps you organize resources, monitor income and spending, and make educated financial choices. It offers a framework for monitoring cash flow, identifying areas of overspending or cost reductions, and defining financial objectives.
2. developing a Budget: Guide readers through the process of developing a complete budget. Start by identifying distinct budget categories, such as income, operational costs, capital expenditures, and contingency

reserves. Encourage readers to acquire previous financial data and use it as a basis for projecting future costs and income.

3. Sales and Revenue projecting: Discuss approaches for projecting sales and revenue. Explain the value of market research, industry trends analysis, and consumer insights in developing accurate revenue estimates. Guide readers on how to create realistic sales objectives including seasonality or market swings, and factor in any projected changes in price or product/service offerings.

4. Expense Management: Help readers learn how to manage and control spending properly. Encourage them to review historical spending, find areas of possible cost reductions, and prioritize important expenditures. Emphasize the necessity of reviewing costs periodically and changing the budget as required to achieve financial stability.

5. Cash Flow Management: Explain the relevance of controlling cash flow to support corporate operations. Educate readers about cash inflows and outflows, and assist them in predicting and sustaining positive cash flow. Provide recommendations for improving cash flow, such as negotiating advantageous payment terms with suppliers, motivating early customer payments, or investigating financing alternatives during cash flow shortfalls.

6. Financial Ratios and Key Performance Indicators (KPIs): Introduce readers to crucial financial measures and KPIs that assist in analyzing the financial health and performance of an organization. Explain popular ratios like gross profit margin, net profit margin, return on investment (ROI), and debt-to-equity ratio. Show how these ratios give insights into profitability, efficiency, and overall financial stability.

7. Monitoring and Adjusting the Budget: Stress the significance of frequently evaluating the budget and making appropriate modifications. Guide readers on how to evaluate actual financial outcomes versus planned amounts and examine discrepancies. Explain the importance of finding and correcting budget deviations early to preserve financial control.

8. Contingency Planning: Emphasize the necessity for contingency planning in budgeting and financial forecasts. Encourage readers to account for unforeseen occurrences or changes in market circumstances by putting up contingency reserves. Discuss techniques for risk reduction and financial resilience, such as diversifying income sources or having a cash reserve for emergencies.

9. getting Professional Financial Guidance: Advise readers to consider getting professional financial guidance as required. Discuss the role of accountants, financial advisers, or business consultants in offering assistance on budgeting, financial forecasting, and overall financial management. Highlight the significance of their skills in managing difficult financial concerns and maintaining regulatory compliance.

10. frequent Financial Reviews: Encourage readers to do frequent financial reviews to analyze their business's financial performance. Discuss the necessity of studying financial statements, profit and loss reports, and balance sheets to acquire insights into the business's financial health. Guide them on how to understand financial data and make educated choices based on the results.

By highlighting the significance of budgeting and financial forecasting, you enable readers to make solid financial choices, manage resources wisely, and handle possible financial issues. Providing practical ideas, examples, and templates will further aid readers in applying budgeting and financial forecasting approaches in their enterprises.

B. Bookkeeping and Accounting Basics:
Managing Financial Records and Ensuring Accuracy

Accurate bookkeeping and accounting are vital for ensuring financial transparency, complying with rules, and making educated company choices. This portion of your book focuses on the basic concepts of bookkeeping and accounting. Let's review the fundamental features of bookkeeping and accounting basics:

1. Introduction to Bookkeeping: Explain the objective of bookkeeping and its function in financial management. Discuss the necessity of keeping structured financial records, monitoring income and spending, and ensuring compliance with tax and regulatory regulations.

2. Chart of Accounts: Introduce the notion of a chart of accounts, which is a classified list of all the financial accounts utilized in a firm. Discuss the many forms of accounting, such as assets, liabilities, equity, income, and costs. Explain how the chart of accounts creates the framework for documenting financial transactions properly.

3. Double-Entry Bookkeeping: Explain the concepts of double-entry bookkeeping, which stipulates that every financial transaction has two equal and opposing impacts on the accounts. Discuss the use of debits and credits to record transactions in multiple accounts and preserve the balance between them.

4. Recording Transactions: Guide readers on how to record financial transactions correctly. Explain the process of journaling transactions, including identifying the accounts impacted, establishing the proper debit and credit amounts, and recording the transaction details. Provide examples and activities to enhance comprehension.

5. General Ledger: Discuss the general ledger, which acts as a central repository for all the accounts in a corporation. Explain how transactions from the journals are posted to the associated accounts in the general ledger. Highlight the necessity of keeping correct and up-to-date ledger entries.

6. Trial Balance: Explain the objective of a trial balance and how it helps assure the correctness of the accounting process. Guide readers on how to construct a trial balance by listing all the accounts and their related debit and credit amounts. Emphasize the necessity of balancing debits and credits to discover problems.

7. Financial Statements: Introduce readers to the major financial statements, such as the income statement, balance sheet, and cash flow statement. Explain the purpose of each statement and how they give useful insights into the financial performance and position of an

organization. Discuss the necessity of drafting these statements appropriately and frequently.

8. Cash vs. Accrual Accounting: Discuss the distinctions between cash-basis and accrual-basis accounting. Explain the merits and cons of each option and help readers pick whether the approach is right for their company. Discuss the notion of revenue recognition and the need to match costs with revenues.

9. Managing Accounts Payable and Receivable: Guide readers on how to successfully manage accounts payable (money owed to suppliers) and accounts receivable (money owed by consumers). Discuss the significance of timely invoicing, monitoring payments, and following up on delayed payments. Provide recommendations for maximizing cash flow via smart administration of these accounts.

10. Financial Software and Tools: Discuss the significance of utilizing accounting software and technologies to simplify bookkeeping procedures. Introduce major accounting software solutions and discuss their features and advantages. Highlight the benefits of adopting technology to automate processes, create financial reports, and preserve accurate financial records.

By giving a complete review of bookkeeping and accounting essentials, readers will get a firm foundation in maintaining their business's financial records effectively and evaluating the financial health of their endeavor. Encourage readers to adopt appropriate bookkeeping procedures from the outset and consider hiring professional accounting aid as required.

C. Pricing Strategies and Profit Margins:
Determining the Right Price for Your Products or Services

Pricing your items or services effectively is a vital part of company success. This portion of your book dives into different pricing methods and how to calculate and maintain profit margins successfully. Let's analyze the essential components of pricing strategies and profit margins:

1. Understanding Pricing Fundamentals: Introduce readers to the essential ideas of pricing, including cost-based pricing, value-based pricing, and competition-based pricing. Discuss the elements that impact price choices, such as manufacturing costs, market demand, consumer perception, and competitive environment.

2. Cost Analysis and Profit Margin Calculation: Guide readers on how to undertake a detailed cost analysis to establish the real expenditures involved in manufacturing and delivering their goods or services. Explain how to determine profit margins by subtracting the total expenses from the selling price and expressing it as a percentage.

3. Markup vs. Margin: Differentiate between markup and margin, since they are sometimes misconstrued. Explain that markup is the amount added to the cost price to arrive at the selling price, while margin is the percentage of the selling price that indicates profit.

4. Pricing Strategies: a. Cost-Plus Pricing: Discuss the cost-plus pricing method, where a defined percentage of profit is added to the cost of manufacturing a product or providing a service. Highlight the ease and predictability of this technique but also its limits in capturing the genuine value experienced by consumers. a. Value-Based Pricing: Explain the value-based pricing strategy, which decides the price based on the perceived value of the product or service to the client. Discuss the significance of knowing consumer wants, benefits, and willingness to pay for the value offered. c. Psychological Pricing: Introduce readers to psychological pricing tactics, such as charm pricing (using prices ending in 9), prestige pricing (setting higher prices to give a sense of high quality), and bundling (combining many goods at a reduced price). Explain how these methods impact customer behavior and purchase choices. d. Dynamic Pricing: Discuss dynamic pricing, where prices change depending on criteria like demand, time of day, season, or consumer group. Explain the benefits of dynamic pricing in optimizing income but also advise readers about possible obstacles in implementation.

5. Competitor study: Stress the need to perform a competitor study to understand the pricing landscape in the industry. Encourage readers to examine their rivals' pricing methods, product offers, and positioning. Guide them on how to utilize this information to make intelligent price choices and distinguish their services.

6. Pricing for Different Market Groups: Discuss the notion of pricing discrimination, when different client groups are charged different rates depending on their willingness to pay. Guide readers on how to discover and target distinct market niches with specialized pricing methods to optimize income.

7. Promotions and Discounts: Discuss the usage of promotions, discounts, and special offers as part of the pricing strategy. Highlight their efficacy in attracting consumers, generating sales, and clearing surplus inventory. Emphasize the necessity of properly planning and monitoring the effect of promotions on overall profitability.

8. Monitoring and Adjusting Pricing Strategies: Advise readers to frequently assess the success of their pricing strategies and make modifications as appropriate. Encourage them to utilize key performance indicators (KPIs) including gross profit margin, sales volume, and customer feedback to analyze price choices' effectiveness.

By taking readers through different pricing methods and profit margin calculations, you enable them to make educated price choices that line with their company objectives and give value to consumers while guaranteeing profitability. Remind them that pricing is not a one-time choice, but a continuing process that needs frequent assessment and modification.

D. Cash Flow Management:
Ensuring a Healthy Cash Flow for Business Operations

Managing cash flow is crucial for the financial health and profitability of any firm. This portion of your book focuses on efficient cash flow management, offering readers with ideas and ways to maintain a healthy cash flow. Let's study the major components of cash flow management:

1. Importance of Cash Flow Management: Explain the relevance of cash flow management in corporate operations. Discuss how cash flow influences the capacity to fulfill financial commitments, invest in growth prospects, and manage unforeseen costs. Emphasize that prosperous organizations might still experience cash flow issues if finances are not handled efficiently.

2. Cash Flow Statement: Introduce readers to the cash flow statement, a financial statement that records the input and outflow of cash over a given time. Explain the three primary areas of the cash flow statement: operating operations, investment activities, and financing activities. Help readers understand how to interpret the statement and find areas of concern.

3. Cash Flow Forecasting: Guide readers on how to build a cash flow forecast, which forecasts future cash inflows and outflows based on past data and expected activities. Discuss the necessity of precise forecasting to predict cash flow shortfalls or surpluses. Provide practical advice for establishing realistic cash flow estimates.

4. Managing Accounts Receivable: Discuss ways for efficiently managing accounts receivable, which are payments owed by customers. Encourage readers to create clear payment conditions, invoice quickly, and follow up on missed payments. Provide help in developing credit rules, handling collections, and maintaining strong customer relationships.

5. Controlling Accounts Payable: Explain the necessity of controlling accounts payable, which are the payments owing to suppliers and vendors. Discuss tactics for maximizing payment terms, securing beneficial discounts, and maintaining vendor relationships. Encourage readers to strike a balance between timely payments and maintaining financial flow.

6. Inventory Management: Discuss the effect of inventory on cash flow and the need for efficient inventory management. Guide readers on how to assess inventory levels, minimize overstocking or understocking, and

apply just-in-time inventory techniques. Emphasize the relevance of matching inventory levels with customer demand to improve cash flow.

7. Expense Management: Stress the significance of limiting spending to ensure a healthy cash flow. Encourage readers to frequently examine spending, seek cost-saving options, and negotiate favorable terms with suppliers. Discuss approaches for controlling variable and fixed costs, such as assessing cost structures and maximizing resource usage.

8. Financing choices: Introduce readers to several financing choices that may assist in managing cash flow changes. Discuss short-term funding possibilities including lines of credit, company credit cards, and invoice finance. Explain the advantages and drawbacks of each choice and urge readers to carefully examine their demands and financial capacity.

9. Cash Flow Monitoring and Analysis: Guide readers on how to monitor and evaluate cash flow regularly. Discuss the utilization of essential financial measures including cash conversion cycle, days sales outstanding, and liquidity ratios. Provide practical advice for evaluating cash flow patterns, spotting possible concerns, and taking proactive efforts to rectify them.

10. Emergency Fund and Contingency Planning: Highlight the need to build an emergency fund to cover unanticipated costs or cash flow shortfalls. Discuss contingency planning and the importance of company insurance in managing financial risks. Encourage readers to devote a percentage of their revenues to develop a cash reserve for emergencies.

By offering readers with realistic solutions for cash flow management, you enable them to maintain a healthy financial position, navigate cash flow difficulties, and make educated choices to promote company development and stability. Remind them that cash flow management involves frequent attention and aggressive efforts to guarantee continued financial health.

E. Managing Business Debts and Expenses:
Strategies for Effective Debt and Expense Management

Proper management of corporate debts and costs is vital for preserving financial stability and optimizing profitability. This portion of your book focuses on giving readers ideas and tactics to efficiently manage their debts and reduce spending. Let's study the major components of controlling company debts and expenses:

1. Assessing Current Debts and Expenses: Guide readers on performing a detailed review of their present obligations and spending. Encourage them to develop a detailed inventory of all outstanding bills, including loans, credit cards, and other financial responsibilities. Similarly, counsel them to assess their recurrent and discretionary spending to discover areas where cost-saving solutions might be adopted.

2. Prioritizing Debt Repayment: Discuss the significance of prioritizing debt repayment to decrease interest expenses and increase cash flow. Help readers comprehend alternative debt repayment techniques, such as the snowball approach (paying off bills with the lowest sums first) or the avalanche method (prioritizing loans with the highest interest rates). Provide help on building a debt payback plan and adhering to it.

3. Negotiating with Creditors: Encourage readers to proactively engage and negotiate with their creditors when suffering financial troubles. Discuss options for renegotiating payment terms, interest rates, or payback schedules. Advise readers to be upfront about their financial condition and suggest viable repayment alternatives that correspond with their existing cash flow.

4. Expense Reduction Techniques: Provide real advice and approaches for decreasing corporate expenditures without sacrificing quality or productivity. Discuss solutions such as: • Conducting frequent expenditure audits to detect unneeded or excessive spending.
   - Negotiating better arrangements with suppliers and vendors.
   - Implementing energy-efficient methods to cut electricity bills.
   - Streamlining operations and removing redundancies.
   - Leveraging technology to automate processes and cut manual labor expenses.

5. Applying Cost Control Strategies: Guide readers on applying efficient cost control strategies to monitor and manage their spending. Discuss the significance of making budgets, managing costs, and frequently

checking financial data. Encourage readers to include key stakeholders in expenditure reduction initiatives and build a culture of cost-consciousness inside the business.

6. Exploring Debt Consolidation Options: Introduce readers to the notion of debt consolidation, which includes consolidating various loans into a single loan with more favorable conditions. Discuss the pros and concerns of debt consolidation and suggest readers analyze their financial circumstances and speak with financial advisors before pursuing this option.

7. Creating a Contingency Fund: Stress the significance of building a contingency fund to manage unforeseen costs or financial crises. Encourage readers to put away a percentage of their earnings as savings to establish a buffer against unanticipated occurrences. Discuss the advantages of having a contingency fund and give help in setting a suitable savings objective.

8. Getting Professional Financial Counsel: Emphasize the significance of getting professional financial counsel for managing company debts and spending. Recommend readers to meet with accountants, financial experts, or business consultants who may give individualized counsel and expertise targeted to their unique situations.

9. Monitoring and Adjusting Strategies: Remind readers of the need to regularly review and alter their debt and spending control tactics. Encourage them to frequently check their financial records, analyze the success of their efforts, and make necessary modifications to keep on course toward their financial objectives.

By offering readers with solutions for successful debt and spending management, you enable them to take charge of their financial condition, minimize debt loads, and improve their business's profitability. Remind readers that controlling debts and costs takes continual attention and a proactive strategy to maintain long-term financial security.

CHAPTER 11

SCALING AND GROWTH

A. Assessing Growth Opportunities:
Identifying and Evaluating Paths for Business Expansion

As firms mature, seeking expansion prospects becomes vital for long-term success. In this portion of your book, readers will discover how to examine and evaluate numerous development prospects. Here are the important components to cover:

1. The Importance of Growth: Begin by underlining the relevance of growth for firms. Explain that growth opens up new markets, boosts revenue and profitability, draws investors, and gives chances for innovation and development. Emphasize that identifying growth prospects is a critical step in building a roadmap for company success.
2. Market study: Guide readers on how to perform a complete market study to find prospective development possibilities. Explain the significance of knowing market trends, consumer demands, and competitive

landscapes. Encourage readers to utilize resources like market research, questionnaires, and industry publications to acquire helpful insights.

3. Expansion within the Current Market: Discuss the prospects for expansion inside the present market. Guide readers on how to identify untapped client niches, unmet demands, and emerging trends within their sector. Provide methods for growing market share, boosting product offerings, and building customer connections.

4. Geographic growth: Explore the potential of geographic growth. Help readers learn how to analyze new areas or nations for market potential, cultural fit, regulatory issues, and competitive dynamics. Discuss tactics for entering new markets, including alliances, acquisitions, or setting up local operations.

5. Product Diversification: Introduce readers to the notion of product diversification as a growth strategy. Explain how increasing the product or service portfolio might attract new consumers and enhance income sources. Discuss strategies for gauging market demand, performing product research, and introducing new offers effectively.

6. Strategic Partnerships and Alliances: Discuss the possible advantages of strategic partnerships and alliances as a growth strategy. Guide readers on how to discover acceptable partners, create mutually profitable partnerships, and exploit combined capabilities to reach new markets or access new resources.

7. Acquisitions and Mergers: Explore the potential of expansion via acquisitions or mergers. Discuss the factors for finding possible acquisition targets, completing due diligence, and integrating acquired enterprises effectively. Highlight the possible benefits of utilizing existing infrastructure, customer base, or intellectual property via strategic acquisitions.

8. Franchising and Licensing: Explain the notion of franchising or licensing as a growth strategy. Discuss how readers may analyze the possibility of franchising their company model or licensing their goods or services. Provide insights into the legal and practical elements involved in franchising or licensing agreements.

9. Technology and Innovation: Highlight the importance of technology and innovation in driving corporate success. Discuss the significance of adopting new technology, investing in research and development, and keeping ahead of industry trends. Encourage readers to research disruptive technology or novel business strategies that may provide new growth prospects.

10. Financial evaluation: Stress the need to undertake a financial evaluation to determine the feasibility and profitability of expansion options. Guide readers on how to examine the financial implications of alternative growth methods, including revenue predictions, cost considerations, and return on investment computations.

11. Risk Analysis: Remind readers to do a comprehensive risk analysis while considering growth potential. Discuss the risks and problems connected with each growth plan, such as market volatility, regulatory impediments, operational complications, or financial limits. Provide advice on risk reduction and contingency preparation.

12. Developing a Growth Plan: Assist readers in establishing a development strategy based on their evaluated prospects. Encourage them to develop clear objectives, establish meaningful tasks, and allocate resources wisely. Emphasize the need to continually assess and modify the growth strategy to changing market circumstances.

By providing readers with a methodical methodology to examine development prospects, you enable them to make educated choices and design plans that correspond with their company objectives. Remind readers that progress involves careful preparation, continual monitoring, and an adaptive mentality to grasp opportunities and overcome problems along the way.

B. Expanding Your Product/Service Offerings:
Strategies for Diversification and Innovation

Expanding your product/service offerings is a vital growth strategy that helps you attract more clients, improve income streams, and remain competitive in the market. In this portion of your book, readers will learn about practical ways to extend their product or service portfolio. Here are the important components to cover:

1. Assessing Customer demands: Encourage readers to undertake rigorous market research and customer analysis to uncover unmet demands and gaps in the market. Help them realize the value of getting input from current customers and new target groups to acquire insights into their preferences and problem concerns.

2. Product/Service Innovation: Discuss the value of innovation in increasing offerings. Encourage readers to think creatively and explore methods to better their present goods or services or build whole new ones. Highlight the advantages of keeping ahead of trends, adopting new technology, and always upgrading to satisfy shifting client expectations.

3. Market Research and Validation: Guide readers on doing market research and validation to guarantee that their new product/service ideas correspond with market demand. Help students comprehend the value of evaluating market trends, assessing competition, and verifying their ideas via surveys, focus groups, or prototype testing.

4. Product/Service Development Process: Provide readers with a step-by-step tutorial on the product/service development process. Explain the significance of defining clear goals, creating a timeframe, and allocating resources wisely. Discuss approaches like as agile development or iterative prototyping to guarantee an efficient and customer-focused approach.

5. Pricing and Positioning: Help readers comprehend the implications of pricing and positioning while extending their offers. Discuss techniques for establishing competitive pricing that represent the value proposition of the new product/service. Guide readers on placing their products in the market, considering criteria such as target audience, distinction, and perceived value.

6. Launch and Marketing plan: Assist readers in building an effective launch and marketing plan for their new product/service. Discuss numerous channels and strategies, including digital marketing, conventional advertising, public relations, and social media, to raise

awareness and attract consumers. Emphasize the significance of generating an appealing message and interacting with the target audience.

7. Upselling and Cross-Selling: Explain the advantages of utilizing current customer ties to extend offers. Guide readers on using upselling and cross-selling methods to drive clients to acquire extra products/services or upgrade to higher-value alternatives. Provide examples and best practices for successful upselling and cross-selling.

8. Strategic Partnerships and Collaborations: Explore the possibility of strategic partnerships and collaborations to extend services. Encourage readers to establish mutually beneficial connections with complementary firms or industry specialists. Discuss how partnerships may help increase product/service reach, tap into new markets, and exploit common resources and expertise.

9. Testing and Iteration: Emphasize the necessity of testing and iterating new solutions depending on customer input and market reaction. Encourage readers to acquire data and insights from early customers, monitor key performance metrics, and make required modifications to enhance their offers for success.

10. Managing Growth and Scalability: Discuss the issues of managing growth and scalability while increasing product/service offerings. Help readers comprehend the need for scalability planning, operational efficiency, and resource allocation to meet rising demand and retain customer satisfaction.

11. ongoing Improvement: Highlight the value of ongoing improvement in maintaining success with expanding options. Encourage readers to acquire client input, watch market trends, and innovate consistently to remain ahead of the competition and keep relevance in the industry.

By leading readers through successful techniques for increasing their product/service offerings, you enable them to diversify their company, attract new clients, and drive growth. Remind readers that growth takes careful planning, market validation, and a customer-centric strategy to create value and long-term success.

C. Geographic Expansion and Market Penetration:
Strategies for Reaching New Markets

Expanding your firm into new geographic locations is an exciting opportunity for development and market penetration. In this portion of your book, readers will learn about techniques and considerations for effectively extending their firm into new areas. Here are the important components to cover:

1. Market Research and Analysis: Explain the necessity of performing extensive market research and analysis when contemplating geographic growth. Guide readers on how to analyze the potential of new markets, considering elements such as population demographics, consumer behavior, cultural differences, competitiveness, and regulatory environment.

2. Market entrance techniques: Discuss several market entrance techniques that readers might explore, such as direct sales, partnerships, joint ventures, franchising, or licensing. Explain the benefits and disadvantages connected with each technique and help readers pick the best-suited plan based on their company objectives and available resources.

3. Localization and Adaptation: Highlight the need to adjust goods, services, and marketing methods to meet the new market's cultural and customer preferences. Encourage readers to perform market-specific research and consider elements like language, culture, buying patterns, and local legislation when personalizing their services.

4. Distribution and Logistics: Guide readers on building up effective distribution channels and logistics networks to assist their regional development. Discuss aspects such as transportation, warehousing, inventory management, and fulfillment to guarantee smooth operations and timely delivery of products/services.

5. Competitive Analysis: Help readers comprehend the competitive environment in the new market. Encourage them to perform a detailed study of local rivals, their strengths, shortcomings, and market

positioning. Provide advice on distinguishing their products and building a competitive edge to effectively enter the market.

6. price and Localization: Discuss price methods that match with the local market. Help readers comprehend the elements that impact price, such as local buying power, competition, and cost structures. Guide them on modifying pricing tactics to match local market expectations while retaining profitability.

7. Marketing and Promotion: Assist readers in building efficient marketing and promotional plans for their regional development. Discuss the value of localized marketing efforts, branding, advertising, and client acquisition methods relevant to the target market. Encourage the use of market-specific messages and cultural sensitivity to successfully connect with the local audience.

8. Legal and Regulatory Considerations: Highlight the necessity of knowing the legal and regulatory requirements in the new market. Guide readers on doing due diligence to guarantee compliance with local laws, permits, licenses, tax requirements, and intellectual property protection. Encourage them to obtain legal representation or engage local specialists to understand the legal situation.

9. Partnerships and Networks: Discuss the possible advantages of developing partnerships or using local networks to aid market entrance and growth. Guide readers on discovering and building contacts with local distributors, suppliers, industry alliances, or government bodies that may give vital insights and help.

10. Risk Assessment and Mitigation: Help readers analyze and reduce risks connected with regional growth. Discuss aspects such as government stability, economic climate, currency changes, logistical problems, and cultural barriers. Encourage readers to establish contingency plans and risk mitigation methods to overcome possible problems.

11. Scalability and Operations: Guide readers on growing their operations to match the needs of the new market. Discuss concerns such as personnel, infrastructure, supply chain management, and customer

support to ensure a smooth transition and maintain high service standards.

12. Continued Monitoring and Adaptation: Emphasize the need for continual monitoring and adaptation in the new market. Encourage readers to collect feedback, evaluate key performance measures, and remain sensitive to market changes. Highlight the necessity for flexibility and agility in altering plans depending on market circumstances and client preferences.

By offering readers with ideas and insights on global development and market penetration, you enable them to explore new markets, extend their client base, and drive company success. Remind readers that effective growth takes careful planning, adaption to local markets, and a customer-centric strategy to fulfill the particular demands of each geographic location.

D. Franchising and Licensing Options:
Expanding Your Business Through Partnerships

Franchising and licensing provide unique potential for company development by enabling entrepreneurs to utilize existing brands, business models, and processes. In this portion of your book, readers will learn about the advantages, concerns, and actions involved in franchising or licensing their firm. Here are the important components to cover:

1. Understanding Franchising and Licensing: Introduce readers to the ideas of franchising and licensing. Explain the difference between the two approaches, where franchising entails a more extensive agreement that includes brand utilization, operational rules, and continuing assistance, while licensing offers rights to utilize intellectual property or particular products/services under specified conditions.

2. Evaluating Franchise/Licensing Potential: Help readers decide if franchising or licensing is right for their firm. Discuss elements such as the distinctiveness of their company model, scalability, operational

processes, and market demand. Guide readers on examining their willingness to share power and engage with partners.

3. Franchise/licensing Development: Outline the step-by-step process of building a franchise or licensing program. Discuss the main components, such as developing extensive paperwork (Franchise Disclosure Document or Licensing Agreement), deciding the extent of the relationship, providing clear norms and objectives, and implementing training and support mechanisms.

4. Legal and Regulatory Compliance: Emphasize the necessity of complying with legal and regulatory standards when engaging in franchise or licensing agreements. Explain the legal duties, such as disclosure obligations, trademarks, intellectual property protection, and compliance with local laws. Encourage readers to obtain legal assistance to ensure compliance with applicable rules.

5. locating and Selecting Franchisees/Licensees: Provide help in locating and selecting qualified franchisees or licensees. Discuss the necessity of choosing people or firms that connect with the brand values, have the required skills and resources, and exhibit a commitment to the success of the collaboration. Guide readers on doing rigorous due diligence and screening procedures.

6. Training and assistance: Highlight the value of providing thorough training and continuous assistance to franchisees or licensees. Discuss the need to share operating systems, best practices, and marketing tactics to guarantee uniformity across all sites. Help readers comprehend the necessity for constant communication and support mechanisms for resolving problems and establishing a collaborative partnership.

7. Financial Considerations: Discuss the financial elements of franchising or licensing. Guide readers on selecting proper franchise fees, royalties, or licensing fees to guarantee profitability for both sides. Encourage readers to build financial models and predictions to examine the possible returns and expenses involved with growing via franchising or licensing.

8. Brand Management and Quality Control: Stress the necessity of maintaining brand consistency and quality control across all franchise or license sites. Explain the importance of enforcing brand standards, performing frequent inspections, and developing performance assessment methods to defend the reputation and integrity of the organization.

9. Resolving disagreements and Disputes: Provide recommendations on how to address disagreements or disputes that may develop within the franchising or licensing arrangement. Encourage readers to develop clear conflict resolution channels and, if required, pursue mediation or arbitration processes to settle conflicts and preserve a good working relationship.

10. International Franchising and Licensing: Briefly touches on the concerns and obstacles involved with international franchising or licensing. Highlight the necessity for market research, recognizing cultural differences, adjusting company models, complying with international legislation, and creating strong local alliances to guarantee effective development into overseas markets.

By digging into franchising and licensing opportunities, you enable readers to explore other avenues to company development and utilize partnerships to increase their brand and reach. Remind readers that careful preparation, good relationships, and continued support are crucial for successful franchising or licensing initiatives.

E. Strategic Partnerships and Collaborations:
Unlocking Growth via Collaboration

Strategic partnerships and collaborations may be significant vehicles for company success, enabling entrepreneurs to harness complementary resources, knowledge, and networks. In this portion of your book, readers will learn about the advantages, considerations, and techniques for building strategic partnerships and collaborations. Here are the important components to cover:

1. Understanding Strategic Partnerships and Collaborations: Introduce readers to the notion of strategic partnerships and collaborations. Explain how these connections entail mutually advantageous agreements between two or more organizations to pursue similar objectives, such as increasing market reach, acquiring new technology, sharing expenses, or boosting product/service offerings.

2. Identifying Partnership Opportunities: Help readers uncover prospective cooperation possibilities by examining their company requirements and objectives. Discuss the significance of selecting partners that match their strengths and limitations, have similar values and goals, and may bring unique resources or competencies that strengthen their competitive edge.

3. creating Trust and Rapport: Highlight the value of creating trust and rapport with prospective partners. Discuss the value of networking, attending industry events, and creating contacts that provide the framework for successful partnerships. Encourage readers to participate in open and honest communication to foster trust and alignment.

4. identifying Partnership Objectives and Terms: Guide readers on properly identifying partnership objectives, roles, duties, and expectations. Discuss the need to draft a formal agreement or memorandum of understanding that describes the scope of the partnership, resource contributions, decision-making procedures, and governance structures.

5. Collaboration Models: Explore several cooperation models that readers might explore, such as joint ventures, co-marketing campaigns, co-development of products/services, research collaborations, or strategic alliances. Explain the benefits, difficulties, and possible hazards connected with each model and help readers select the most suited method for their firm.

6. utilizing Complementary Resources: Illustrate the advantages of utilizing complementary resources via partnerships. Discuss how firms might exchange information, skills, client bases, distribution networks, technology, or physical assets to support mutual development and

innovation. Guide readers on recognizing their unique resources and promoting them as important contributions to future collaborations.

7. cooperation in Research and Development: Discuss the prospects for cooperation in research and development (R&D). Highlight the advantages of pooling resources, sharing intellectual property, and partnering with other firms, academic institutions, or research groups to expedite innovation and bring innovative products/services to market.

8. Managing Partnership Relationships: Provide information on efficiently managing partnership relationships. Discuss the need for frequent communication, shared planning, and periodic review of partnership effectiveness. Help readers comprehend the necessity for flexibility, compromise, and conflict resolution processes to sustain a healthy and effective relationship.

9. Mitigating Risks and Legal Concerns: Highlight the need to manage risks and address legal concerns in partnerships. Encourage readers to undertake due diligence on possible partners, safeguard intellectual property, and develop confidentiality and conflict resolution channels. Advise readers to obtain legal assistance when establishing partnership agreements to ensure compliance with applicable laws and regulations.

10. Monitoring and evaluating collaboration performance: Guide readers on monitoring and evaluating the performance of their collaboration activities. Discuss key performance indicators (KPIs) that may be used to measure the impact and efficacy of cooperation. Encourage readers to get input from stakeholders, monitor results, and make appropriate modifications to enhance collaboration outcomes.

11. Case Studies and Success Stories: Share real-world case studies and success stories of firms that have achieved considerable growth via strategic partnerships and collaborations. Highlight the techniques, obstacles experienced, and lessons gained from these cases to motivate readers and give practical insights.

By examining the domain of strategic partnerships and collaborations, you enable readers to explore mutually beneficial ties that may promote innovation, growth, and long-term success for their enterprises. Remind readers that creating good relationships needs proactive networking, clear communication, and common objectives to produce a win-win scenario for all parties involved.

CHAPTER 12

OVERCOMING CHALLENGES AND RISKS

A. Identifying Common Business Challenges:

Navigating Obstacles on the Path to Success

Running a company comes with its fair share of hurdles and barriers. In this portion of your book, you will assist readers in anticipating and solving frequent business obstacles. Here are the important components to cover:

1. Market Volatility: Discuss the issue of handling market volatility, including varying consumer demand, changing economic situations, and competitive landscapes. Provide tactics for adjusting to market changes, such as broadening product offerings, performing market research, and being adaptive.

2. Financial Management: Address the difficulty of financial management, including cash flow management, budgeting, and obtaining money. Offer ideas for good financial planning, managing costs, optimizing earnings, and obtaining financial help when required.

3. Hiring and maintaining Talent: Explore the problems of recruiting and maintaining competent people. Discuss successful recruiting techniques, building a healthy work culture, giving professional development opportunities, and adopting retention programs to attract and retain top personnel.

4. Competition: Help readers navigate the competitive environment by analyzing their rivals, recognizing their unique value proposition, and implementing strategies to distinguish their goods or services. Emphasize the necessity of constant market study and keeping ahead of industry trends.

5. developing and Growth: Discuss the issues involved with developing a firm, such as managing greater operations, maintaining quality control, and acquiring new resources. Provide advice on strategic planning, process optimization, and effective delegation to promote successful growth.

6. Technology Adoption: Address the problem of accepting and exploiting technology to boost corporate operations and competitiveness. Discuss the pros and hazards of embracing new technology, implementing digital solutions, and remaining up-to-date with industry changes.

7. Legal and Regulatory Compliance: Highlight the obstacles to addressing legal and regulatory obligations relevant to the business and area. Provide an overview of typical compliance challenges, such as licenses, permits, intellectual property, data protection, and employment requirements. Encourage readers to get legal counsel and implement systems for continuous compliance.

8. Customer Satisfaction and Retention: Discuss the significance of satisfying customer expectations and overcoming customer service difficulties. Provide techniques for enhancing customer satisfaction,

managing complaints, and creating long-term customer connections via great service and tailored experiences.

9. Time Management and Job-Life Balance: Address the difficulty of reconciling job commitments with personal well-being. Offer practical advice for successful time management, prioritizing, and building boundaries to create a good work-life balance.

10. adaptation and Resilience: Highlight the need for adaptation and resilience in the face of unanticipated situations, such as economic downturns, natural catastrophes, or technology upheavals. Share experiences of firms that successfully handled hard times and share techniques for developing resilience and adjusting to change.

11. Emotional Well-being and Stress Management: Discuss the relevance of emotional well-being and stress management for entrepreneurs. Offer ideas for self-care, stress reduction techniques, and accessing support networks to sustain mental and emotional wellness.

By tackling typical business difficulties, you educate readers to proactively anticipate and overcome barriers on their entrepreneurial path. Remind readers that obstacles are chances for development and learning, and with the correct mentality and tactics, they can overcome any roadblock that comes their way.

B. Managing and Mitigating Risks:
Safeguarding Your Business and Minimizing Potential Pitfalls

Running a company contains inherent risks, but proactive risk management is vital to limiting their effect. In this portion of your book, you will walk readers through appropriate risk management tactics. Here are the important components to cover:

1. Risk Assessment: Teach readers how to identify and analyze hazards related to their sector and company operations. Discuss the necessity of doing a complete risk assessment, including identifying possible hazards, analyzing their probability and potential effect, and classifying risks based on severity.

2. Risk Mitigation Techniques: Provide readers with a selection of risk mitigation techniques to assist them in proactively addressing identified issues. This may involve creating safety rules, making contingency plans, diversifying suppliers, gaining insurance coverage, or adopting redundancy measures. Emphasize the necessity of continually analyzing and upgrading risk mitigation methods as the firm changes.

3. Financial Risk Management: Explore financial risks that firms encounter, such as cash flow changes, economic downturns, or unplanned costs. Offer techniques for financial risk management, such as having a cash reserve, diversifying income sources, monitoring important financial KPIs, and getting expert financial guidance as required.

4. Legal and Compliance Risks: Highlight the necessity of knowing and complying with relevant laws, regulations, and industry standards. Discuss approaches to minimize legal and compliance concerns, such as consulting legal counsel, performing frequent compliance audits, establishing strong data protection measures, and keeping correct records.

5. Cybersecurity and Data Protection: Address the increased danger of cyber-attacks and data breaches. Educate readers about recommended practices for cybersecurity, including utilizing secure networks and passwords, frequently upgrading software, teaching personnel about data protection, and having a data breach response strategy in place.

6. Operational Risks: Discuss operational risks that might affect company continuity, such as equipment failure, supply chain interruptions, or personnel mistakes. Offer techniques for controlling operational risks, such as instituting quality control procedures, developing backup systems, diversifying suppliers, and giving continual training to personnel.

7. Reputation and Brand Risks: Highlight the necessity of controlling reputation and brand risks. Discuss the effect of unfavorable press, consumer complaints, or social media reactions. Provide direction on developing a strong brand reputation via constant delivery of excellent

products/services, good customer communication, and proactive reputation management.

8. Crisis Management: Help readers establish a crisis management strategy to successfully react to unforeseen occurrences or crises. Discuss the necessity of creating communication lines, assigning key decision-makers, and detailing step-by-step processes to manage crises immediately and openly.

9. Risk Monitoring and Evaluation: Emphasize the necessity of continuing risk monitoring and evaluation. Encourage readers to periodically examine their risk management methods, update risk registers, and keep them aware of new risks or industry trends that may affect their firm. Foster a culture of constant development and adaptation.

10. Learning from Mistakes and Failures: Highlight the significance of learning from prior mistakes and failures. Encourage readers to accept setbacks as great learning experiences, reflect on lessons gained, and apply them to future risk management methods. Share experiences of successful entrepreneurs who overcame failures and utilized them as stepping stones to attain greater success.

By providing readers with effective risk management techniques, you provide them with the skills to detect, mitigate, and react to risks proactively. Remind readers that risk management is an ongoing process that involves vigilance, adaptation, and a commitment to continuous development.

C. Adapting to Market Changes:
Staying Agile in a Dynamic Business Landscape

The business environment is continuously developing, and successful entrepreneurs must be proficient at responding to market developments. In this portion of your book, you will instruct readers on how to navigate and adapt to market dynamics efficiently. Here are the important components to cover:

1. Monitoring Market Trends: Emphasize the necessity of remaining updated about industry trends, customer behavior, and upcoming market prospects. Encourage readers to perform frequent market research, follow industry journals, attend relevant conferences, and participate in networking to acquire insights on market trends.

2. consumer Feedback and Insights: Discuss the relevance of getting consumer feedback and utilizing it as a significant source of information for understanding market demands and preferences. Guide readers on how to obtain client feedback using surveys, interviews, or social media listening, and how to assess and utilize the information acquired to enhance their products/services.

3. Competitive Analysis: Highlight the necessity of knowing and monitoring the competitive environment. Teach readers how to do a competitive analysis, including identifying major rivals, analyzing their strengths and shortcomings, and utilizing that knowledge to develop their company strategy and products.

4. Embracing Innovation: Encourage readers to embrace innovation as a strategy for keeping ahead of market developments. Discuss the advantages of embracing new technology, exploring new business models, and creating a culture of innovation inside their firm. Provide instances of firms that effectively embraced innovation and earned a competitive advantage.

5. Flexibility and Agility: Emphasize the necessity for flexibility and agility in reacting to market developments. Guide readers on how to construct a responsive and adaptable organizational structure, where decision-making procedures are simplified, and teams are empowered to swiftly make essential adjustments.

6. Product/Service Evolution: Discuss the need to regularly review and develop products/services to satisfy changing market expectations. Encourage readers to request client feedback, undertake product/service evaluations, and make required upgrades or revisions to remain relevant and competitive.

7. Strategic Partnerships and Collaborations: Highlight the advantages of developing strategic partnerships and collaborations to respond to market developments. Discuss how partnerships may help increase reach, access new markets, harness complementary resources, and provide fresh views to business difficulties.

8. Digital Transformation: Address the rising role of digital transformation in adjusting to market developments. Discuss the possibilities of digital technologies, such as e-commerce, social media, and automation, to promote company agility, improve consumer engagement, and create operational efficiency.

9. Continuous Learning and Skill Development: Encourage readers to engage in their own learning and skill development to remain informed about industry trends and market developments. Recommend resources such as books, online courses, seminars, or industry certifications that may assist entrepreneurs in developing new skills and expertise.

10. Risk-Taking and Adaptability: Stress the necessity of adopting reasonable risks and being adaptive in the face of market changes. Encourage readers to be open to experimenting, learn from setbacks, and pivot their tactics as required to exploit new possibilities or handle altering client needs.

By instructing readers on how to adapt to market changes, you enable them to remain ahead of the curve and proactively react to growing client wants and industry trends. Remind readers that adaptation and agility are vital skills for long-term company success and development.

D. Learning from Failures and Setbacks:
Turning Setbacks into Stepping Stones

Failure and setbacks are an essential part of the entrepreneurial path, but they may also serve as great learning opportunities. In this portion of your book, you will instruct readers on how to accept mistakes, learn from setbacks, and utilize them as stepping stones toward future success. Here are the important components to cover:

1. Embracing a Growth mentality: Encourage readers to embrace a growth mentality, which views failures and setbacks as chances for development and learning. Discuss the significance of reframing failures as stepping stones and seeing setbacks as temporary hurdles that can be overcome with patience and tenacity.

2. Analyzing Failure: Teach readers how to assess failures and setbacks objectively. Guide them through a process of self-reflection and assessment of the causes that contributed to the failure. Encourage readers to identify lessons learned, opportunities for development, and insights acquired from the experience.

3. Identifying fundamental reasons: Help readers uncover the fundamental reasons for their failures or setbacks. Encourage them to go beyond surface-level concerns and delve deeper to identify underlying reasons that led to the result. Emphasize the necessity of resolving these core reasons to avoid such errors in the future.

4. Adjusting methods: Guide readers on how to alter their methods based on lessons learned from failures. Encourage them to iterate and develop their company concepts, products/services, marketing techniques, or operational procedures. Highlight the significance of flexibility and agility in reacting to feedback and market circumstances.

5. Seeking Feedback and Guidance: Encourage readers to seek feedback and guidance from mentors, peers, or industry experts. Discuss the significance of acquiring multiple viewpoints and harnessing the experiences of others who have had similar situations. Emphasize the necessity of developing a support network that can give direction during challenging times.

6. creating Resilience: Discuss the necessity of creating resilience to bounce back from failures and setbacks. Provide tactics for growing resilience, such as practicing self-care, creating a positive mentality, setting realistic expectations, and celebrating little triumphs along the road.

7. Persistence and Perseverance: Highlight the relevance of persistence and perseverance in the face of adversity. Share experiences of

successful entrepreneurs who met difficulties but persevered, modified their ideas, and finally found success. Inspire readers to remain devoted to their objectives and not allow failures to stop them from following their business aspirations.

8. Turning Setbacks into chances: Encourage readers to consider setbacks as chances for creativity and progress. Discuss instances of firms that changed failures into new company concepts, better procedures, or inventive solutions. Guide readers on how to recognize chances for development and innovation emerging from setbacks.

9. Cultivating a Learning Culture: Discuss the value of developing a learning culture inside their firm. Encourage readers to establish an atmosphere where failures are considered as learning opportunities and team members are encouraged to discuss and learn from their errors. Promote continuing professional growth and constant progress.

10. Celebrating triumphs: Remind readers to enjoy their triumphs, no matter how minor. appreciate that setbacks and failures are part of the road, but accomplishments deserve acknowledgment and celebration. Encourage readers to reflect on their achievements, appreciate their development, and utilize these successes as inspiration to continue moving ahead.

By instructing readers on how to learn from mistakes and setbacks, you enable them to convert problems into opportunities for development and progress. Remind readers that failures are not the end but rather stepping stones on their route to business success.

E. Building Resilience and Perseverance:
Navigating Challenges with Strength and Determination

Resilience and endurance are key attributes for entrepreneurs to handle the ups and downs of the business journey. In this portion of your book, you will instruct readers on how to develop resilience, foster persistence, and conquer challenges. Here are the important components to cover:

1. Understanding Resilience: Define resilience and its relevance in entrepreneurship. Explain that resilience is the capacity to bounce back

from setbacks, adapt to change, and retain a positive outlook in the face of adversity.

2. Developing Emotional Intelligence: Discuss the importance of emotional intelligence in fostering resilience. Teach readers to identify and control their emotions effectively, as well as develop empathy and strong interpersonal skills to handle hard circumstances and form solid connections.

3. Cultivating a Positive mentality: Emphasize the value of a positive mentality in conquering problems. Guide readers on strategies to build positivity, such as practicing appreciation, reframing problems as opportunities, and retaining optimism even in the face of failures.

4. Building a Support Network: Highlight the necessity of surrounding oneself with a supporting network of mentors, peers, and advisers. Encourage readers to seek assistance, input, and support from this network at hard times. Discuss the advantages of joining entrepreneurial groups, networking events, or mentoring programs.

5. Managing Stress and Self-Care: Discuss the effect of stress on resilience and suggest solutions for stress management. Guide readers on the significance of self-care, including physical activity, a good diet, sufficient rest, and participating in activities that promote relaxation and well-being.

6. Learning from Setbacks: Teach readers how to learn from setbacks and errors. Emphasize the significance of self-reflection and recognizing lessons learned from each struggle. Encourage readers to consider setbacks as chances for development and to change their plans appropriately.

7. Setting Realistic Expectations: Help readers develop realistic expectations and recognize that the entrepreneurial path is filled with ups and downs. Discuss the value of patience and tenacity, as well as the necessity to adjust plans as required.

8. Developing Problem-Solving abilities: Guide readers on how to acquire excellent problem-solving abilities. Teach students to approach

obstacles with a solution-oriented perspective, break down big problems into smaller doable tasks, and seek new solutions.

9. Resilient Communication: Highlight the necessity of efficient communication during stressful times. Teach readers how to communicate freely and frankly with team members, investors, and stakeholders to manage expectations and develop trust.

10. Celebrating Tiny Wins: Encourage readers to appreciate tiny triumphs along the way. Remind them that each step forward, no matter how tiny, is progress. Celebrating milestones and appreciating successes may give motivation and reinforce a feeling of accomplishment.

11. Persevering in the Face of Failure: Discuss the role of tenacity in business. Share experiences of great entrepreneurs who endured several setbacks yet continued to accomplish their objectives. Encourage readers to regard failure as a stepping stone rather than a wall and to keep driving despite setbacks.

12. Learning to Adapt: Emphasize the necessity for adaptation in the ever-changing corporate context. Teach readers to accept change, anticipate market developments, and proactively alter their strategy to remain relevant and competitive.

By coaching readers on growing resilience and persistence, you provide them with the mentality and skills essential to overcome obstacles and failures. Remind readers that resilience is not an intrinsic attribute but may be cultivated through practice and self-reflection. Encourage them to embrace the business adventure with tenacity, dedication, and a never-give-up mentality.

CHAPTER 13

EXIT STRATEGIES AND SUCCESSION PLANNING

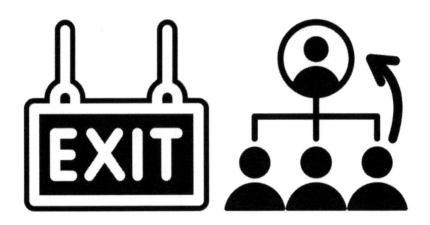

A. Understanding Exit Strategies:

Planning for the Future of Your Business

Exit plans play a key part in the long-term success of a corporation. In this portion of your book, you will discuss numerous exit methods accessible to entrepreneurs and assist readers on how to prepare for the ultimate transition or exit from their organization. Here are the important components to cover:

1. Importance of Exit Strategies: Explain the relevance of having an exit plan in place from the early stages of beginning a firm. Discuss how an exit plan offers clarity, optimizes value, and assures a seamless transition for the firm and its stakeholders.

2. frequent Exit methods: Provide an overview of the most frequent exit methods accessible to entrepreneurs, such as:

a. Sale of the company: Discuss the process of selling a company to a third party, including preparing the business for sale, appraisal methods, discovering possible purchasers, negotiating approaches, and finalizing the deal.

b. Initial Public Offering (IPO): Explain the process of bringing a private firm public through an IPO, including the benefits, problems, and regulatory requirements involved.

c. Merger or Acquisition: Explore the possibility of merging with or being acquired by another firm, including the advantages, considerations, and integration process.

d. Succession preparation: Discuss the need to prepare for a seamless transfer of ownership and management to a successor, whether it's a family member, an important employee, or an outsider applicant. Cover the stages involved in succession planning, including identifying and grooming possible successors, legal and financial issues, and defining a schedule for the transfer.

e. Liquidation: Address the possibility of closing the firm and selling off its assets to repay creditors or distribute residual monies to shareholders. Discuss the procedures involved in the liquidation process and the possible ramifications for stakeholders.

3. Factors Influencing Exit Strategy Selection: Help readers comprehend the elements that might impact their choice of departure strategy. Discuss topics such as personal ambitions, financial aspirations, market circumstances, industry developments, and the general health and potential of the firm.

4. moment the departure: Guide readers on how to establish the proper moment for their departure plan. Discuss issues such as market circumstances, company performance, growth prospects, and personal preparation. Emphasize the necessity of being proactive and preparing ahead rather than being pushed into an unforeseen departure.

5. Professional help: Advise readers on the advantages of getting professional help from business experts, lawyers, and accountants while formulating and implementing their exit plans. Explain how these

specialists may give essential knowledge, direction, and support throughout the process.

6. Communicating the Exit plan: Discuss the necessity of honest communication with stakeholders, including workers, partners, customers, and investors, regarding the selected exit plan. Explain the need to manage expectations and preserve company continuity throughout the transition.

7. Tax and Legal Considerations: Highlight the tax and legal issues connected with potential departure plans. Encourage readers to engage with tax consultants and legal specialists to guarantee compliance and improve their financial results.

8. Post-departure Plans: Guide readers on preparing for life after the departure, whether it means pursuing new initiatives, enjoying retirement, or exploring other personal and professional prospects. Discuss the significance of having personal objectives, managing finances, and keeping a sense of purpose outside the company.

By giving readers a full grasp of exit plans, you enable them to make educated choices regarding the future of their organization. Encourage readers to treat their departure plan as a proactive and purposeful process, enabling a seamless transition and maximizing the value they have generated.

B. Selling Your Business:
Maximizing Value and Navigating the Sales Process

Selling a company may be a challenging and significant time for an entrepreneur. In this portion of your book, you will assist readers through the process of selling their company, delivering essential insights and tactics to optimize value and manage the sales process. Here are the important components to cover:

1. Preparing for the Sale: Explain the necessity of preparing the company for sale to optimize its worth. Discuss techniques such as arranging financial documents, executing a comprehensive company assessment,

and resolving any operational or legal difficulties that might affect the sale.

2. Valuing Your Firm: Explore numerous ways of valuing a firm, including financial statements analysis, market comparables, and discounted cash flow analysis. Help readers understand the aspects that determine the worth of their company and give help in determining a fair and appealing asking price.

3. Finding prospective Buyers: Discuss several channels and tactics for finding prospective buyers, such as using personal networks, engaging business brokers, utilizing internet markets, or participating in industry-specific networks and events. Offer recommendations for discovering qualified and eligible purchasers who connect with the business's purpose and values.

4. Marketing and Presenting Your Company: Guide readers on how to properly promote and show their company to prospective consumers. Discuss the need to establish a convincing sales memorandum or pitch deck that shows the business's unique value proposition, financial performance, growth potential, and competitive edge. Offer advice on presenting financial and operational data clearly and transparently.

5. Negotiating the Deal: Provide readers with negotiating methods and tools to manage the deal-making process. Discuss essential negotiating factors, such as pricing, conditions, contingencies, and non-compete clauses. Offer advice for maintaining a collaborative and productive attitude while arguing for the seller's interests.

6. Due Diligence: Explain the due diligence process, during which prospective purchasers extensively analyze the business's financials, operations, legal papers, and other pertinent information. Guide readers on how to prepare for and handle due diligence, emphasizing the necessity of keeping accurate and well-documented records.

7. Structuring the Sale: Explore alternative transaction forms and their effects, such as asset sales, stock sales, or mergers. Discuss the benefits and drawbacks of each structure and their influence on taxes, obligations, and continued engagement in the firm.

8. Legal and Financial Considerations: Emphasize the need to contact legal and financial specialists to advise sellers through the legal and financial elements of the transaction. Discuss the necessity for extensive sale agreements, non-disclosure agreements, and the participation of escrow agents to guarantee a smooth and secure transaction.

9. Transition and Post-Sale Planning: Help readers negotiate the post-sale transition phase, including the transfer of ownership, management duties, and customer interactions. Discuss ways for handling the emotional and practical elements of moving out of the company, including preparing for personal and financial objectives beyond the sale.

10. Exiting with honesty: Encourage readers to value honesty and openness throughout the sales process. Emphasize the significance of maintaining open communication, honoring duties to workers, customers, and suppliers, and establishing a good legacy for the firm.

By providing readers with a complete guide on selling their company, you enable them to make educated choices and maximize value during this crucial transition. Remind readers that selling a company involves careful planning, preparation, and coordination with specialists to ensure a good end.

C. Succession Planning and Business Continuity:
Securing the Future of Your Business

Succession planning is vital for facilitating the seamless succession of leadership and sustaining corporate continuity. In this portion of your book, you will lead readers through the process of succession planning, stressing the significance of preparing for the future and ensuring the long-term survival of their organization. Here are the important components to cover:

1. The Importance of Succession Planning: Explain why succession planning is vital for the long-term success of a firm. Discuss the hazards associated with a lack of succession planning, such as leadership vacuums, loss of institutional knowledge, and possible disruption to

operations. Highlight the advantages of a well-executed succession plan, including preserving the business's heritage, maintaining stability, and encouraging expansion.

2. Identifying Succession Candidates: Guide readers on how to identify possible successors inside the firm. Discuss aspects including talents, expertise, cultural fit, and long-term commitment to the organization. Encourage readers to consider both internal candidates, such as important workers or family members, and outsider candidates who may provide new viewpoints and skills.

3. creating Succession Candidates: Provide direction on creating and preparing possible successors for leadership posts. Discuss tactics such as mentorship, job rotation, training programs, and exposure to diverse sectors of the company. Emphasize the significance of cultivating talent and establishing a culture of ongoing learning and growth.

4. Transition Planning: Help readers build a complete transition plan that includes the schedule, responsibilities, and processes involved in the succession process. Discuss the necessity of incorporating all stakeholders, including the existing company owner, successors, important workers, and external consultants, in the planning and implementation of the transition. Address possible issues and concerns, such as managing expectations and balancing the interests of numerous stakeholders.

5. Communicating the Succession Plan: Guide readers on how to successfully communicate the succession plan to all important stakeholders, including workers, customers, suppliers, and investors. Discuss the necessity of honest and timely communication to retain confidence and promote a seamless transition. Address frequent concerns and give strategies for addressing possible opposition or ambiguity.

6. Legal and Financial Considerations: Explain the legal and financial elements of succession planning, including the transfer of ownership, tax consequences, and the function of legal arrangements such as buy-sell agreements or shareholder agreements. Encourage readers to obtain

help from legal and financial specialists to guarantee compliance with applicable legislation and to maximize the financial results of the succession.

7. Business Continuity Planning: Highlight the necessity of business continuity planning in connection with succession planning. Discuss the procedures involved in constructing a business continuity plan, including identifying vital functions, preparing contingency plans for anticipated interruptions, and guaranteeing the availability of key resources. Emphasize the necessity to continuously evaluate and update the business continuity strategy to adapt to changing conditions.

8. Evaluating Succession strategy efficacy: Guide readers on how to assess the efficacy of their succession strategy over time. Discuss the necessity of frequent assessments, feedback loops, and revisions to ensure that the plan stays aligned with the developing requirements of the organization.

9. Addressing Unforeseen Circumstances: Prepare readers for unforeseen occurrences or circumstances that may compel an unplanned succession. Discuss ways for coping with unexpected sickness, incapacity, or death of the company owner or key workers. Emphasize the necessity of having contingency plans in place to minimize interruption and preserve company continuity.

By providing readers with a thorough guide to succession planning and business continuity, you enable them to ensure the future of their organization and prevent possible risks. Remind readers that succession planning is a continual process that involves careful thought, teamwork, and adaptation. Encourage them to start early and to employ the experience of legal, financial, and business consultants to establish a solid and successful succession plan.

D. Retirement and Legacy Planning:
Securing Your Future and Leaving a Lasting Impact

Retirement planning is a vital component of entrepreneurship, guaranteeing financial stability and a seamless transition into the next phase of life. In this portion of your book, you will lead readers through the process of retirement and legacy planning, highlighting the necessity of preparing for retirement and leaving a lasting influence via their company. Here are the important components to cover:

1. Understanding Retirement objectives: Help readers establish their retirement objectives and ambitions. Encourage them to visualize their ideal retirement lifestyle, incorporating variables such as financial independence, travel, hobbies, and humanitarian endeavors. Discuss the significance of having precise and measurable objectives to drive their retirement planning process.

2. analyzing Financial Fitness: Guide readers in analyzing their financial fitness for retirement. Discuss critical concerns such as analyzing retirement savings, investments, and assets, as well as projecting future needs and income sources. Encourage readers to interact with financial advisors to do a full retirement analysis and assess their financial requirements during retirement.

3. Retirement Savings Techniques: Provide information on successful retirement savings techniques, such as individual retirement accounts (IRAs), 401(k) plans, and other investment vehicles. Discuss the significance of consistent contributions, diversification, and frequent examination of investment portfolios. Explain numerous retirement savings strategies and their tax consequences, letting readers make educated decisions about maximizing their retirement funds.

4. shifting Ownership and Leadership: Help readers through the process of shifting ownership and leadership of their firm upon retirement. Discuss possibilities such as selling the firm, passing it on to family members or workers, or pursuing mergers and acquisitions. Emphasize the need to plan early, including important stakeholders, and evaluate the financial and operational ramifications of each decision.

5. Estate Planning and Money Transfer: Guide readers in building an estate plan to enable the seamless transfer of their money and assets. Discuss the necessity of making a will, establishing trusts, and designating beneficiaries. Encourage readers to cooperate with estate planning

specialists to handle tax implications, reduce possible conflicts, and preserve their assets.

6. Philanthropy and Giving Back: Explore options for readers to create a lasting influence via philanthropy and giving back. Discuss tactics such as founding philanthropic foundations, building endowments, or supporting organizations aligned with their principles. Provide advice on successful philanthropic planning and the possible advantages of incorporating charity into their retirement and legacy plans.

7. recording Your Business Heritage: Help readers maintain their business heritage by recording their entrepreneurial experience and lessons acquired. Discuss the value of recording critical company processes, strategies, and milestones in a standardized way. Encourage readers to consider building a company legacy plan that includes written documents, images, films, and personal tales that may be shared with future generations or the greater business community.

8. Personal Fulfillment in Retirement: Address the non-financial components of retirement planning, stressing the significance of preserving personal fulfillment and a feeling of purpose. Discuss ideas for pursuing hobbies, participating in lifelong learning, volunteering, or exploring new endeavors after retirement. Encourage readers to think about their own beliefs and objectives to construct a retirement plan that extends beyond financial stability.

9. Continual Review and Adjustment: Emphasize the necessity for continuing assessment and modification of retirement and legacy plans. Discuss the need to modify plans to changing circumstances, market conditions, and personal aspirations. Encourage readers to frequently connect with financial and legal advisors to ensure their retirement plan stays aligned with their shifting requirements.

By providing readers with a thorough guide to retirement and legacy planning, you empower them to safeguard their financial future and make a lasting effect via their business activities. Remind readers that retirement planning is a continuous process that involves proactive involvement and a comprehensive approach. Encourage them to start early, seek expert counsel, and consider the larger legacy they desire to leave behind as they move into the next phase of their life.

CONCLUSION

Empowering You to Build Your Business Legacy

Congratulations on concluding "The Dummies Guide to Starting Your Own Business." Throughout this book, we have been on a journey together, exploring the exciting and hard world of entrepreneurship. We have covered everything from comprehending the core of entrepreneurship to constructing a sound company strategy, handling legal issues, and implementing efficient marketing and sales techniques. We dug into financial management, operations, and development, and we even addressed retirement and legacy planning.

Now, when you finish this book, I want to leave you with an encouraging message: You can construct your company legacy. Each step you take, and each choice you make, puts you closer to accomplishing your ambitions and leaving a lasting effect on the world. You have received a plethora of information and insights that will serve as a firm basis for your business path.

Remember, entrepreneurship is not only about financial success; it's about following your passion, generating value for others, and leaving a good impression on society. It's about accepting difficulties, adjusting to change, and continually learning and improving. It's about developing meaningful connections with consumers, workers, and stakeholders. And it's about resilience, persistence, and never losing sight of your goal.

As you begin on your business road, remain loyal to yourself and your principles. Embrace creativity, embrace failure as a stepping stone to success, and embrace the pleasure and satisfaction that comes from making something of your own. Surround yourself with a supportive network, seek direction from mentors, and never hesitate to ask for assistance when required.

Remember that success is not defined just by financial gains, but also by the good influence you have on people and the legacy you leave behind. Whether it's generating employment, fixing social issues, or inspiring future generations of entrepreneurs, your company may be a force for good.

So, go ahead with confidence, passion, and drive. Embrace the difficulties, cherish the wins, and learn from every encounter. Your path as an entrepreneur will include ups and downs, but remember that you have the knowledge, abilities, and perseverance to conquer every challenge that comes your way.

Thank you for joining me on this fascinating voyage. I believe in you and your potential to build something extraordinary. Now, it's time to transform your goals into reality, leaving behind a great and lasting company legacy that will inspire people for centuries to come.

Printed in Great Britain
by Amazon

42696470R00090